"何以中国"文物考古大展系列

龙腾中国

红山文化古国文明

"The Essence of China," an Exhibition Series of Cultural Relics and Archaeological Achievements

Legends of Dragon

The Ancient Civilization of Hongshan Culture

［目 录］

02 敬天　Worship of Heaven

总　序

参天之木，必有其根；怀山之水，必有其源。

习近平总书记强调，中华文明源远流长、博大精深，是中华民族独特的精神标识，是当代中国文化的根基，是维系全世界华人的精神纽带，也是中国文化创新的宝藏。在漫长的历史进程中，中华民族以自强不息的决心和意志，筚路蓝缕，跋山涉水，走过了不同于世界其他文明体的发展历程。

为加快上海建设具有世界影响力的社会主义现代化国际大都市，以中华优秀传统文化创造性转化、创新性发展，更好地回应时代之变、人民之需，上海博物馆"大博物馆计划"应时而生。"大博物馆计划"之"大"，重在配置大资源，吸引大流量，打造大IP，促进大科研，推动上海博物馆建设成为"中国特色世界一流"的博物馆，赋能上海城市软实力的全面提升。作为"大博物馆计划"展陈的重要组成部分，"何以中国"文物考古大展系列联手国内各大博物馆，充分挖掘优质丰富的馆藏资源和最新考古发现，展示中华文明起源、发展和灿烂成就，彰显博物馆在中华文明传承中的重要作用，着力做好"以物论史"和"以史增信"两篇大文章。

所谓"以物论史"，重在着眼上海实际，聚焦文物考古重点项目，深度参与中华文明探源工程，深化研究中华文明起源、特质和形态，大力推动具有中国特色、中国风格、中国气派的考古学的上海卓越实践，努力破解历史之谜，回答重大历史问题。所谓"以史增信"，重在深化文旅融合，坚持以文塑旅、以旅彰文，高水平做好考古挖掘阐释和文博立体展示，大力推动"让文物活起来"，增强全球叙事能力，讲好精彩上海故事，传播展示中华文明的悠久历史、人文底蕴和时代风采，弘扬中华文明蕴含的全人类共同价值，向世界展现可信、可爱、可敬的中国形象。

文物是发展的见证，历史是时代的回响，它们是时光与万物的共振，也是人生与天地的交响。

忆往昔，波澜壮阔，历久弥坚，令人荡气回肠。

展未来，意气风发，谱写新篇，中华再度辉煌！

上海市文化和旅游局局长
上海市文物局局长
钟晓敏

General Preface

A tree growing upward to the heavens has its roots well into the earth. A river running by a range of mountains has its source long long away.

President Xi Jinping has underlined the fact for us that the Chinese civilization is both long and deep. Indeed, the length and depth is a unique feature of the Chinese spirit, the basis for present-day Chinese culture, the spiritual ties between the Chinese all over the world, and the powerhouse for China's cultural innovation. Over the long course of history, the Chinese nation, with its unfailing determination and will power, has undergone epic hardships and difficulties to discover its own path of self-development, which proves to be different in essence from those of the other great civilizations.

Now, the Shanghai Museum has, in order to help make Shanghai a socialist cosmopolis with international prominence and to update itself creatively and develop itself innovatively so that it may with greater efficiency answer the calls of the times and meet the needs of the people, launched with pride the Project of Great Museums. The greatness lies in the allocation of great resources, attraction of great internet traffic, creation of great intellectual property, and promotion of great research, with an eye to making the Shanghai Museum a world-class museum with Chinese characteristics and to helping enhance the soft power of Shanghai comprehensively. As an integral part of the project, "The Essence of China," an exhibition series of cultural relics and archaeological achievements, is based on a constellation of China's great museums, fully taps the rich, quality resources of museum collections and the latest archaeological finds, unveils the origin, growth, and splendid fruits of the Chinese civilization, demonstrates the important role of museums in passing down the priceless cultural treasures of China, and serves as an eloquent footnote to the Materialistic Approach to Historical Studies and to the Enhancement of Faith with Historical Studies.

As to the Materialistic Approach, we shall take into account the actual circumstances of Shanghai, keep our focus upon key projects of cultural relics and archaeology, deepen our commitment to the search for the very origin of the Chinese civilization, further our studies on the conception, distinctiveness, and morphology of the civilization, powerfully endorse the excellent archaeological practices by Shanghai scholars with a specialty, a style, and a splendor that are China's own, endeavor to decipher myths in and provide answers to questions from history. As to the Enhancement of Faith, we shall lay our emphasis on an upgraded integration of cultural exploration and tourism. Indeed, we shall guide the development of our tourism industry with our culture and in the meantime promote our culture by boosting our tourism, interpret archaeological excavations with a greater clarity and display museum exhibits with a greater accessibility, try to the best of our ability to "enliven our cultural relics," improve our narrative caliber in our communication with the world outside, recount the cultural legends of Shanghai more convincingly, display and popularize the long history, the humanistic tradition, and the current achievements of China as a civilization, promote the common values of the human race that are embedded in the Chinese way, and set up to the world an image of China that is worthy of trust, love, and respect.

Cultural relics bear testimony to social progress, and so in the past are found the preludes to the present. They are the sound of the passage of time through everything. They are also the symphony between human and world.

When we look into what lies behind, we see a glory shining beyond the ups and downs that have never beaten us but rather have made us even stronger.

When we look into what lies ahead, we see a fountainhead of energy and motivation that will undoubtedly to victory upon victory bring us as a people known to the world as the Chinese.

Zhong Xiaomin, Director-General
Shanghai Municipal Administration of Culture and Tourism
Shanghai Municipal Administration of Cultural Heritage

致　辞

　　六千年前，当文明的晨曦初照华夏大地，在辽河流域的广袤山川间，一个古老的族群以敬畏之心雕琢玉石，以虔诚之态祭祀天地，在文化的不断碰撞与融合之中，开创了有别于黄河、长江流域文明的红山模式。

　　红山文化，中国北方新石器时代的一颗璀璨明珠，发端于距今6500年前后，并在距今5800年前后进入古国文明阶段。红山文化中发达的祭祀礼仪体系反映了中国文明起源的道路与特点，是中华礼制之源；蜷曲如虹的玉龙则确立了"崇龙尚玉"的精神内核，也为中华民族意识中"龙的传人"找到了根脉。"坛庙冢""玉龙凤"，这些红山文化著名的物质符号由北向南、由东向西、由早及晚，以一种与自然共生的智慧和开放交流的姿态不断扩大，延伸着自己的文化影响力，在不同区域文化之间进行着超越人们想象的交流与传承，形成了中华民族独特的历史文化记忆。

　　天行有常，中华泱泱，"龙腾中国——红山文化古国文明特展"是上海博物馆"何以中国"文物考古大展系列的第四展，以红山考古百年最重要的成果及最新的发现，阐释了红山文化以信仰统一、礼制初成的古国面貌，走出了一条独具特色的文明发展之路，实证了中华民族五千多年的文明史，深刻回答了"何以中国"的历史之问。

　　龙生辽水畔，日出红山后，曙光耀中华！

上海博物馆馆长

褚晓波

Foreword

Some six thousand years ago, as the first light of civilization illuminated the land of China, an ancient people worshipped the heavens and the earth with piety and carved jade with reverence in the Liao River basin. Amidst the continuous collision and integration of cultures, they created the Hongshan model, distinct from the civilizations found in the basins of the Yellow and Yangtze rivers.

The Hongshan Culture, a brilliant pearl of the Neolithic Age in northern China, originated around 6,500 years ago and reached the ancient state phase around 5,800 years ago. Its advanced sacrificial and ritual system reflects the path and characteristics of the origin of Chinese civilization, serving as the source of Chinese rites and ceremonies. The coiled jade dragons established the spiritual core of "dragon veneration and jade appreciation," tracing the roots of the Chinese nation's self-consciousness as "descendants of the dragon." The famous material symbols of Hongshan, such as "altars, temples, and burial mounds" and "dragon- and phoenix-shaped jade artifacts", expanded and extended the culture's influence from north to south and from east to west. With a wisdom of coexistence with nature and an open attitude towards communication, they facilitated exchanges and adoptions among regional cultures, forming a unique cultural memory in the history of the Chinese nation – all beyond our imagination.

Under the vast firmament, China stands as a nation great and glorious. As the fourth in the Shanghai Museum's "The Essence of China" series of archaeological exhibitions, "Legends of Dragon: The Ancient Civilization of Hongshan Culture" interprets the Hongshan Culture's unique path of developing a civilization, characterized by unified beliefs and the initial formation of rites and ceremonies. Through the most important achievements and latest discoveries of a century of Hongshan archaeology, the show provides solid evidence for the over five thousand years' history of Chinese civilization and eloquently answers the ultimate question: What is the essence of China?

The dragon was born by the Liao River, the sun rises behind the Red Mountain, and the dawn shines over China!

Chu Xiaobo
Director of the Shanghai Museum

统一"信仰模式"下的红山社会文明化进程 *

贾笑冰

中国社会科学院考古研究所

在继承本地传统基础上，融合来自其他区域优秀文化因素的红山社会[1]得到了极大发展，继承自本地传统的以刻划或压印"之"字纹为主要纹饰特征的筒形罐仍是红山文化时期最主要的陶器种类，陶器造型丰富多样，彩陶逐渐流行。玉器的出现可以追溯至兴隆洼文化时期，至红山文化时期，玉器的种类和数量都更加丰富。自距今5800年前后的红山文化中期偏晚阶段开始，大型社会公共设施兴建、社会等级分化加剧，红山文化展现出更为强大的社会动员和组织能力，红山"古国"的特征逐步显现，随着"考古中国——红山社会文明化进程研究"工作的开展，新的考古发现为认识红山社会的发展提供了新的资料。

一、社会发展

考古调查显示，红山文化时期遗址数量明显增加，陶片分布密度显示的人口数量也有了极大的增长。随着人口的增加、社会群体规模的扩大，扁平、分散的社会呈现出立体、层级化的特征。

1.区域社会群体的形成

与之前的兴隆洼文化、赵宝沟文化时期[2]相比，红山文化时期的聚落模式发生了明显的变化。

兴隆洼文化时期的遗址规模大体相当，经过系统发掘的白音长汗遗址由两个相邻的环壕聚落组成，共发掘出兴隆洼文化房址40余座，每个环壕内房址约20座[3]；查海遗址发掘出房址50余座[4]，聚落规模与白音长汗遗址大体相当。赵宝沟文化经过系统发掘的仅有赵宝沟遗址，遗址面积9万平方米，发现灰土圈（房址）89个[5]，虽未见环壕，但自然低谷将房址分为两区，布局模式与白音长汗遗址两个环壕区构成的聚落较为相似。这两个时期房址分布较为密集，居住区规模大体相当。

经过系统发掘的红山文化遗址数量不多，只能做大略统计。魏家窝铺遗址环壕内面积9.3万平方米[6]，2009—2011年度发掘共清理房址103座，房址朝向以东南向和西南向为主，另有少量房址朝向为西北向和东北向，其中东南向房址占一半左右。房址与环壕之间的叠压—打破关系表明这些房址应不是同时期使用的，同时使用的房址数量不超过发掘房址数量的一半，可能规模相对较大，房址分布也较为密集。年代稍晚的兴隆沟遗址面积4.1万平方米，环壕内面积近2万平方米[7]，从现有发现情况来看，遗迹密度相对较低。

不同于兴隆洼文化时期大体相近的遗址规模，红山文化遗址的规模差异相对明显，调查发现也显示，中小型遗址的数量相对较多，而少见10万平方米以上的大型遗址[8]，与前两个时期相比，遗址的数量明显增加、分布也更为密集，呈现了遗址聚群分布的特征，在遗址的相对密集分布区之间会存在一定范围的空白区域[9]，这些现象都显示小群体数量的增加和群体规模的扩大。与兴隆洼—赵宝沟文化时期相比，红山文化的社会组织模式发生了明显的变化，兴隆洼文化时期的规模相差不多、相对平等的社群进一步整合成为关系更为密切的大规模社群[10]，社群内部出现了等级分化，小群体并立的扁平化社会向层级化的复杂社会转变。

陶器生产是最易发现的与社会经济联系相关的信息，调查发现，与陶器生产关系最为密切的窑址并未见于所有遗址中，推测可能存在二至三个遗址就近使用一个窑区的现象[11]。目前魏家窝铺、兴隆沟遗址第二地点的发掘资料中皆未见与陶窑相关的信息，西台[12]、上机房营子[13]、四棱山遗址[14]发现了红山文化时期的陶窑，仅西台遗址同时发现了红山文化的居住址，考古发掘资料也显示并非所有的生活居住区都有陶窑。上机房营子遗址陶窑出土筒形罐特征的差异[15]为相邻区域共用陶窑的认识提供了新的证据。日常生活领域的密切联系表明区域群体内部的联系和依赖程度增强，牛河梁遗址筒形器等特殊功能陶器的复杂生产分工则表明更为复杂的社会管理模式已经出现。[16]分布位置相近的聚落组成了功能互补、彼此更加依赖的聚落群，区域社会组织逐渐形成。

牛河梁遗址发现了原料来源复杂、造型多样、制作特征不同的玉器群，表明可能也存在专门的玉器生产地，在区域社会组织的基础上，基于特殊产品的生产和消费，建立起广泛空间内远距离区域社会组织之间的联系。

2.等级秩序的确立

由多个遗址点构成的牛河梁遗址群是区域社会组织已经形成完善的等级秩序的表现，在牛河梁遗址中已经形成了相对明确的等级分化、富与贵的明确区分，确立起相对明确的社会秩序，社会地位的获取更多依赖于在祭祀礼仪体系中的地位而并非社会财富及获取财富的能力。[17]

由于考古发现有限，我们只能通过对资料较多的祭祀礼仪类遗存的分析，在对红山文化存在聚群分布的聚落模式的初步认知的基础上，进一步了解更广阔地域空间范围内的社会组织模式及其影响范围。牛河梁遗址和胡头沟遗址作为结构较为相似、规模略有差异的遗址群，是认识红山文化区域社会关系的最好样本。

牛河梁遗址是由多个遗址点组成的遗址群[18]，目前保护区范围及周边区域发现红山文化遗址点67处；胡头沟遗址群目前仅发掘了胡头沟遗址[19]，调查显示以胡头沟遗址为中心，周边还有多个遗址点[20]，两区域都显示出较为相似的等级分化的特征。胡头沟红山文化墓地的结构、布局与牛河梁遗址基本相同，但在构筑材料及随葬品组合方面显示出与牛河梁遗址之间的等级差异[21]。

牛河梁遗址与胡头沟遗址直线距离约150公里，两地相同的墓地布局规范和统一的等级规范以及区域社会间等级秩序的存在表明，以牛河梁遗址为核心的社会等级秩序已经成为广域空间社会普遍遵守的"共同准

则"。虽然目前尚未发现更为明确的区域间的经济联系，但建立在相同社会规范基础上的统一秩序为红山社会的团结发展奠定了基础。

围绕元宝山遗址开展的考古调查发现了遗址聚群分布的特征[22]，元宝山遗址墓地的结构布局以及出土玉器体量所显示的与牛河梁遗址的等级差也为红山社会广域空间等级秩序的确立提供了新的证据[23]。

二、统一"信仰模式"的构建

红山文化核心分布区域为辽西山地，纵横分布的沟谷限制了遗址的空间扩展范围，"散村"是受山地区域限制的聚落模式，研究发现，聚群分布的遗址之间可能已经在生产生活上出现了一定程度的依赖与联系，但程度较为有限，复杂的生产分工模式和技术的快速发展仍主要体现在以祭祀礼仪活动为核心的特殊产品的生产领域。区域系统性考古调查显示，祭祀礼仪类遗址是区域社会的核心[24]，基于日常生活领域的社会联系不足以建立起广域空间内广泛的社会联系，以祭祀礼仪活动为核心建立起的"信仰模式"成为红山文化统一社会形成的思想基础[25]。

1.以祭祀礼仪活动为核心的等级体系的构建

祭祀礼仪类遗存的等级分化可以为认识牛河梁遗址和胡头沟遗址高等级墓葬之间的等级差异提供依据。

牛河梁遗址是目前发现红山文化规模最大的祭祀礼仪活动中心，其中第一地点的台基建筑群作为牛河梁遗址的重要组成部分，总面积约10万平方米[26]，与目前发现的规模较大的魏家窝铺遗址基本相当，台基上还发现了复杂的祭祀遗迹[27]，这些遗迹表明至少在牛河梁遗址这一时期，红山文化中已经初步形成了"敬天、礼地、法祖"的祭祀礼仪体系。根据祭祀类遗迹残存遗物的种类与特征的不同，祭祀天地的燎祭和瘗埋的遗存还存在进一步分类的可能。"以禋祀祀昊天上帝，以实柴祀日、月、星、辰，以槱燎祀司中、司命、风师、雨师，以血祭祭社稷、五祀、五岳，以貍沉祭山、林、川、泽，以

『何以中国』文物考古大展系列
"The Essence of China," an Exhibition Series
of Cultural Relics and Archaeological Achievements

齻辜祭四方百物。"根据《周礼·春官·大宗伯》的记载，祭天为"祀"、祭地称"祭"，祀天的具体对象可以分为"昊天上帝""日、月、星、辰""司中、司命、风师、雨师"；祭地的对象可以分为"社稷、五祀、五岳""山、林、川、泽"和"四方百物"。根据祭祀对象的不同，祭祀方式上也存在差异。牛河梁遗址发现的特征不同的祭祀坑表明这一时期可能已经初步形成了与《周礼》记载类似的复杂的祭祀活动分类。

除了第一地点之外，第十三地点是一处由中心直径40米的夯土及外围最大直径60米的三重石砌围墙构成的、残高7米的大型单体建筑[28]。虽然现有的资料不足以判定第十三地点的性质和功能，但不同于其他地点的结构显示其在牛河梁遗址群中应是与第一地点较为相似的另一重要的祭祀礼仪活动空间。由第一地点、第十三地点和其他地点以墓葬为主的遗迹共同构成了牛河梁遗址完整的祭祀礼仪活动中心。

目前我们尚未找到胡头沟遗址群的公共礼仪活动空间，东山嘴遗址则可为认识胡头沟遗址群的祭祀活动中心提供信息。东山嘴遗址群初步确定由七处遗址组成，有独立的祭祀遗迹和墓地，其中东山嘴遗址是一处独立的祭祀遗迹[29]，由南侧的圆形祭坛和北侧的长方形建筑基址组成。

与牛河梁遗址相比，东山嘴遗址群的整体规模、祭祀遗迹的种类和面积都相对逊色，其与牛河梁遗址群规模和功能的差异与对文献记载的礼制规范的总结所得出的"祭祀主体的等级不同，祭祀规模场所不同；祭祀对象不同，祭祀方式不同"[30]的结论较为相似，二者共同构成了红山社会完整的祭祀礼仪活动体系，为认识胡头沟遗址与牛河梁遗址所代表的红山社会区域社会群体的关系提供了依据。

2.统一"信仰体系"的形成

与后世规范的礼制特征相比，红山文化中协调人与自然（神）关系与人际关系的礼制仍显示出明显的草创期的特征，从这些特征中我们可以粗略窥见红山社会统一信仰的形成过程。

红山文化的玉礼制尚未形成明确的"六瑞"与"六器"的区分，多见仿生造型的器物，玉器造型多样甚至较少见重复造型。根据器物特征似可以将仿生造型的玉器分为属天和属地两类，在此分类下可以略略领会红山社会玉礼制的规范[31]。玉器种类、造型的多样和复杂不明晰的分类体系显示出明显的礼制初创时期的特征，复杂的"万物有灵"的崇拜开始呈现体系化、秩序化的特征，展现红山文化玉器从早期的装饰品、祭祀或巫术活动的道具到礼制载体的转变路径。

偶像体系的形成与演变则是体现红山文化从本地传统的多元信仰逐渐走向统一的过程的另一重表现。辽西区偶像崇拜的传统可以追溯至兴隆洼文化时期[32]，兴隆洼文化不同区域信仰特征存在一定程度的差异：如西拉木伦河流域主要显示为偶像崇拜，白音长汗[33]、南湾子北[34]等遗址都发现了立置于房址内灶后侧的石雕人像；兴隆洼文化分布区南侧的查海、兴隆洼等遗址中则更多见居室葬。虽然皆为发生在房址内的祭祀活动，但形式和内容存在明显的差别，与之相对应的是房址特征上也存在相应的差异，前者更流行方形石板灶，后者则常见圆形坑灶。二者的对应体现人群与信仰模式之间的相对稳定组合。

赵宝沟文化时期石雕人像继续流行，但分布区域已经不仅限于西拉木伦河流域，石雕人像主要见于滦平后台子遗址[35]，目前尚未发现赵宝沟文化中有居室葬，可能偶像崇拜已经成为这一时期更为主要的原始信仰。

至红山文化时期，雕像的材质种类更为丰富，不仅有石雕人像，还发现了陶塑、泥塑和玉雕人像，人像的体量也出现了两极分化，最小的人像约相当于真人手掌大小，牛河梁遗址"女神庙"出土的大型泥塑人像甚至可以相当于真人三倍[36]。与玉礼器体量的差异体现等级差别一样，偶像的体量同样是"神格"秩序的体现，区域内广泛出现的偶像崇拜在红山文化中出现了秩序化的特征。与玉礼器的特征和分类一样，红山社会将不同区域、可能内涵并不完全相同的偶像信仰整合为一个完整的体系，使之"各安其所"，并非以新的单一信仰来取代旧有的信仰，而是将之体系化、系统化之后，形成了更具包容性的信仰体系。

红山文化在整合区域原始信仰的基础上，构建起新的、更具包容性的社会秩序，为相对分散的红山社会的统一发展奠定了意识形态的基础。

三、精神和制度领域的发展与意义

以祭祀礼仪活动为中心的统一信仰和等级秩序，是红山社会在整合区域小群体社会的基础上实现社会统一发展的基础，其所创立的规范人与神（自然）、人与人之间关系的准则——礼制——对中国传统文化的形成和发展产生了深远的影响，是中国先秦思想发展完善的基础。

1.完备礼制的史前基础

在牛河梁遗址第一地点台基建筑群上发现的"燎祭"遗迹，不同的燎祭遗迹中发现了不同的焚烧物；埋藏有不同种类遗物的"祭祀"坑；与"裸礼"活动遗留近似的器物组合，这些遗迹现象与后世礼制中祭祀对象不同则祭祀方式不同，祭祀对象等级不同则祭品种类、组合不同如出一辙，遗迹与出土遗物的特征似可与文献所记载的对天神、地祇、人鬼的祭祀活动对应，很可能是"燎祭祀天、瘗埋祭地、肆献裸享先王"的源头。西周时期形成的完备的礼制体系中的三个主要祭祀对象，"天神""地祇""人鬼"在红山文化时期已经初步形成。

反映墓主身份地位的玉礼器的分类虽然仍相对较为模糊，尚未形成明确的"以等邦国"和"以礼天地四方"的玉礼器的种类和功能的明确区分，但以之来规范社会关系与《周礼·春官·大宗伯》所载的玉礼制相同。

2."绝地天通"的社会变革

根据《国语·楚语》的记载，上古宗教的发展可以分为"民神不杂""民神杂糅不可方物，夫人作享，家为巫史""使复旧常，（民神）无相侵渎，是谓绝地天通"三个阶段[37]，其所反映的是社会极速发展

过程中，不断秩序化的社会变革。[38]《史记·太史公自序》："昔在颛顼，命南正重以司天，火正黎以司地。唐虞之际，绍重黎之后，使复典之。至于夏商，故重黎氏世序天地。其在周，程伯休甫其后也。当周宣王时，失其官守而为司马氏。"相似论述也见于《国语·楚语下·观射父论绝地天通》。文献记载显示，"绝地天通"并非一次性完成的工作，而是长期开展的"宗教改革"，时间大致可以从红山文化时期复杂社会秩序的形成开始至礼制确立为止。

红山文化时期虽然形成了相对完备的祭祀礼仪体系和社会等级秩序，但这一秩序仍然主要集中于社会上层，分析牛河梁遗址、胡头沟遗址、田家沟遗址的材料可以发现，牛河梁遗址与胡头沟遗址直线距离约150公里，牛河梁遗址与田家沟遗址的直线距离约40公里，发现高等级墓葬的牛河梁遗址与胡头沟遗址的相似性远高于距牛河梁遗址更近的田家沟遗址。社会下层人群的差异性则相对明显，最能反映埋葬风格的墓主头向度在牛河梁、胡头沟遗址有着相同的规律性变化的趋势，田家沟、半拉山遗址在墓葬特征上显示出更为明显的变通性，不仅头向差异大，亦无明显的变化规律，红山社会对下层人群采用了更为包容的策略。

虽然在牛河梁遗址可以发现大型偶像的体量差异与"神格"等级分化的迹象，出现了相对集中的祭祀礼仪活动空间，但小型偶像及区域祭祀活动仍然在社会底层广为流传。兴隆沟遗址房址内出土的陶塑人像，应是兴隆洼文化时期家户内偶像活动的延续，意味着兴隆洼文化时期就已经出现的以个体或家户为主体的仪式活动在红山文化时仍然存在。

红山文化时期出现祭祀活动的两级分化，上层相对集中、规范的祭祀礼仪活动区与传承自更早时期的服务于家户或小区域的仪式行为并存。"绝地天通"所显示的通神的独占和秩序的构建与小区域内传统的巫术活动和偶像崇拜长期共存。红山文化的制度改革开启了"绝地天通"的序幕，为统一社会秩序的构建及红山社会的发展奠定了思想基础。

小结

红山文化以开放、包容的态度将本地文化传统与来自其他区域的优秀文化因素的结合起来，建立起以统一的社会秩序整合起来的具有高度包容性的红山社会。虽然我们现在对红山社会的生业模式、经济发展的了解仍相对有限，日常生活领域信息的相对缺乏影响了对红山文化的社会发展的全面认识，然而，依赖于一定的经济基础实现的制度和精神领域的发展则为认识红山文明的发展程度及文明化的动力机制提供了全新的视角。

与祭祀礼仪活动相关的手工业生产、大型社会公共设施的营建都显示社会在组织和管理能力方面的发展和完善，在整合区域多元信仰传统基础上形成的统一的"信仰模式"是红山社会最为重要的制度创造，是统一的红山社会形成的制度基础。

红山文化不仅继承了辽西区本地的筒形罐传统，更是开启了中国先秦思想史上最重要的社会变革，统一的意识形态和信仰体系的构建为分布地域范围广阔、经济生活依赖不明显的分散性社会的团结发展奠定了思想基础。对区域内流行的多种信仰体系加以整合并使之秩序化的社会制度变革成为红山社会文明化进程的重要动力。

注释：

* 本文为国家社会科学基金中国历史研究院重大历史问题研究专项"牛河梁遗址考古发掘资料整理与研究"（项目批准号：24VLS002）和"考古中国——红山社会文明化进程研究"项目阶段性成果。

1 郭明：《红山——中国文化的直根系》，上海古籍出版社，2022 年。

2 目前研究者对此序列提出了新的观点，然而并未改变三个考古学文化在形成时间上略有先后的认识，且并不影响本文的讨论，在此仍采用传统观点。

3 内蒙古自治区文物考古研究所：《白音长汗——新石器时代遗址发掘报告》，科学出版社，2004 年。

4 辽宁省文物考古研究所：《查海——新石器时代聚落遗址发掘报告》，文物出版社，2012 年。

5 中国社会科学院考古研究所：《敖汉赵宝沟——新石器时代聚落》，中国大百科全书出版社，1997 年。

6 成璟瑭、塔拉、曹建恩、熊增珑：《内蒙古赤峰魏家窝铺新石器时代遗址的发现与认识》，《文物》2014 年第 11 期。

7 中国社会科学院考古研究所内蒙古第一工作队、敖汉博物馆：《内蒙古敖汉旗兴隆沟遗址第二地点红山文化聚落》，《考古学报》2023 年第 4 期。

8 于怀石：《辽宁地区红山文化遗址分布与特征》，《北方文物》2023 年第 4 期。

9 赤峰中美联合考古研究项目：《内蒙古东部（赤峰）区域考古调查阶段性报告》，科学出版社，2003 年；辽宁省文物考古研究所、美国匹兹堡大学人类学系、美国夏威夷大学：《辽宁大凌河上游流域考古调查简报》，《考古》2010 年第 5 期。

10 张弛：《比较视野中的红山社会》，《红山文化研究——2004 年红山文化国际学术研讨会论文集》，文物出版社，2006 年。

11 邵国田：《概述敖汉旗的红山文化遗址分布》，《中国北方古代文化国际学术研讨会论文集》，中国文史出版社，1995 年；刘晋祥、董新林：《燕山南北长城地带史前聚落形态的初步研究》，《文物》1997 年第 8 期。

12 杨虎、林秀贞：《内蒙古敖汉旗红山文化西台类型遗址简述》，《北方文物》2010 年第 3 期；林秀贞、杨虎：《红山文化西台类型的发现与研究》，《考古学集刊》第 19 集，科学出版社，2013 年。

13 内蒙古自治区文物考古研究所、吉林大学边疆考古研究中心：《赤峰上机房营子与西梁》，科学出版社，2012 年。

14 李恭笃、高美璇：《内蒙古敖汉旗四稜山红山文化窑址》，《史前研究》1987 年第 4 期。

15 郭明：《牛河梁遗址红山文化晚期社会的构成》，社会科学文献出版社，2019 年。

16 同注 15。

17 同注 15。

18 辽宁省文物考古研究所：《牛河梁——红山文化遗址发掘报告（1983—2003 年度）》，文物出版社，2012 年。

19 方殿春、刘葆华：《辽宁阜新县胡头沟红山文化玉器墓的发现》，《文物》1984 年第 6 期；方殿春、刘晓鸿：《辽宁阜新县胡头沟红山文化积石冢的再一次调查与发掘》，《北方文物》2005 年第 2 期；赵振生：《辽宁阜新县胡头沟新石器时代红山文化积石冢二次清理研究探索》，《中国考古集成东北卷（5）》，北京出版社，1997 年；辽宁省文物考古研究所：《辽海记忆——辽宁考古六十年重要发现（1954—2014）》，辽宁人民出版社，2014 年。

20 调查在阜新地区牤牛河左岸以胡头沟遗址为中心、半径 15 公里范围内发现了 15 处遗址点，参见郑钧夫、黄婷婷、王滨：《阜新地区红山文化专题调查的方法与实践》，《草原文物》2024 年第 4 期。

21 郭明、盖丽艳：《浅析红山文化的玉礼器与玉礼制》，《北方文物》2023 年第 4 期。

22 内蒙古自治区文物考古研究院：《内蒙古自治区赤峰市敖汉旗元宝山积石冢周边区域考古调查简报》，《草原文物》2024 年第 4 期。

23 内蒙古自治区文物考古研究院：《内蒙古敖汉旗元宝山红山文化积石冢考古发掘取得重大收获》，《中国文物报》2024 年 10 月 11 日，第五版。

24 辽宁省文物考古研究所、匹兹堡大学比较考古学中心：《大凌河上游流域红山文化区域性社会组织》（*Hongshan Regional Organization in the Upper Daling Valley*），匹兹堡，2014 年；辽宁省文物考古研究所、中国人民大学历史学院：《2014 年牛河梁遗址系统性区域考古调查研究》，《华夏考古》2015 年第 3 期。

25 同注 1。

26 中国社会科学院考古研究所、辽宁省文物考古研究院等：《辽宁省凌源市牛河梁遗址第一地点西南建筑群发掘简报》，《考古》2024 年第 5 期。

27 贾笑冰：《红山文化确证中华文明的突出特性》，《历史研究》2024 年第 5 期。

28 同注 18。

29 郭大顺、张克举：《辽宁省喀左县东山嘴红山文化建筑群址发掘简报》，《文物》1984 年第 11 期。

30 同注 27。

31 同注 21。

32 张弛：《不变的信仰与竞争的社会——兴隆洼—红山文化雕塑题材及展演形式》，《文物》2022 年第 7 期。

33 同注 3。

34 党郁：《2016 年内蒙古自治区文物考古研究所考古发现综述》，《草原文物》2017 年第 1 期。

35 承德地区文物保管所等：《河北滦平县后台子遗址发掘简报》，《文物》1994 年第 3 期。

36 辽宁省文物考古研究所：《辽宁牛河梁红山文化"女神庙"与积石冢群发掘简报》，《文物》1986 年第 8 期。

37 陈桐生译注：《国语·楚语下·观射父论绝地天通》，中华书局，2013 年。

38 贾笑冰、郭明：《中国文明起源与"巫教时代"——以辽西区史前文化为中心》，待刊。

022

『何以中国』文物考古大展系列
"The Essence of China:" an Exhibition Series
of Cultural Relics and Archaeological Achievements

The Civilizational Process of the Hongshan Society under a "Unified Belief" Pattern

Jia Xiaobing

The Institute of Archaeology of the Chinese Academy of Social Sciences

Abstract

Inheriting local traditions and integrating excellent cultural elements from other regions, the Hongshan Culture represents the culmination of prehistoric cultures in northern China. Significant social mobilization and organizational capabilities, demonstrated in the construction of large-scale public facilities, and the uniform social order across extensive areas both provide rich material for understanding the Hongshan society in the First Phase of the Ancient State Era. The sophisticated sacrificial rituals, the classification of jade ritual objects, and the consistency of social hierarchy across extensive regions all indicate that the open and inclusive "unified belief" system of the Hongshan society had initially taken shape and became the ideological foundation for social unity and development. The belief system and hierarchical order based on sacrificial rituals are the most important institutional creations of the Hongshan Culture, which had a profound impact on the formation of traditional Chinese governance concepts. Explorations of the civilizational process of the Hongshan society from the perspective of belief and institution will offer new insights into the study of the origins of Chinese civilization.

红山文化代表遗址分布示意图

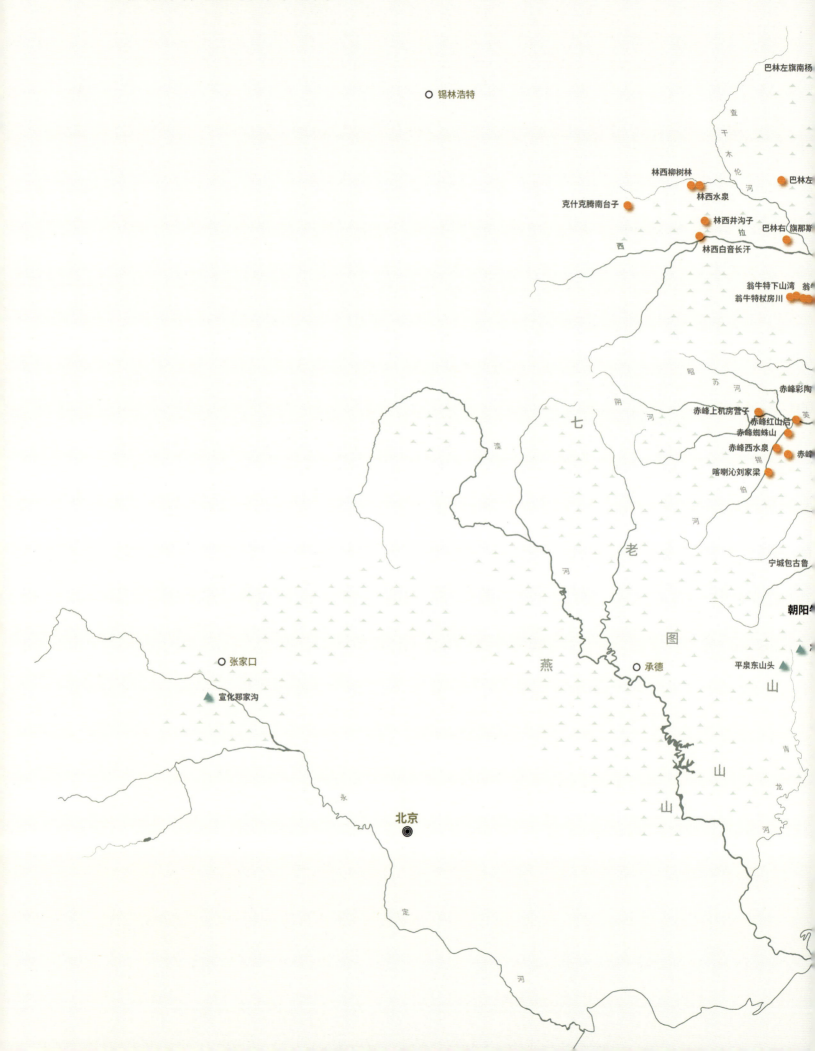

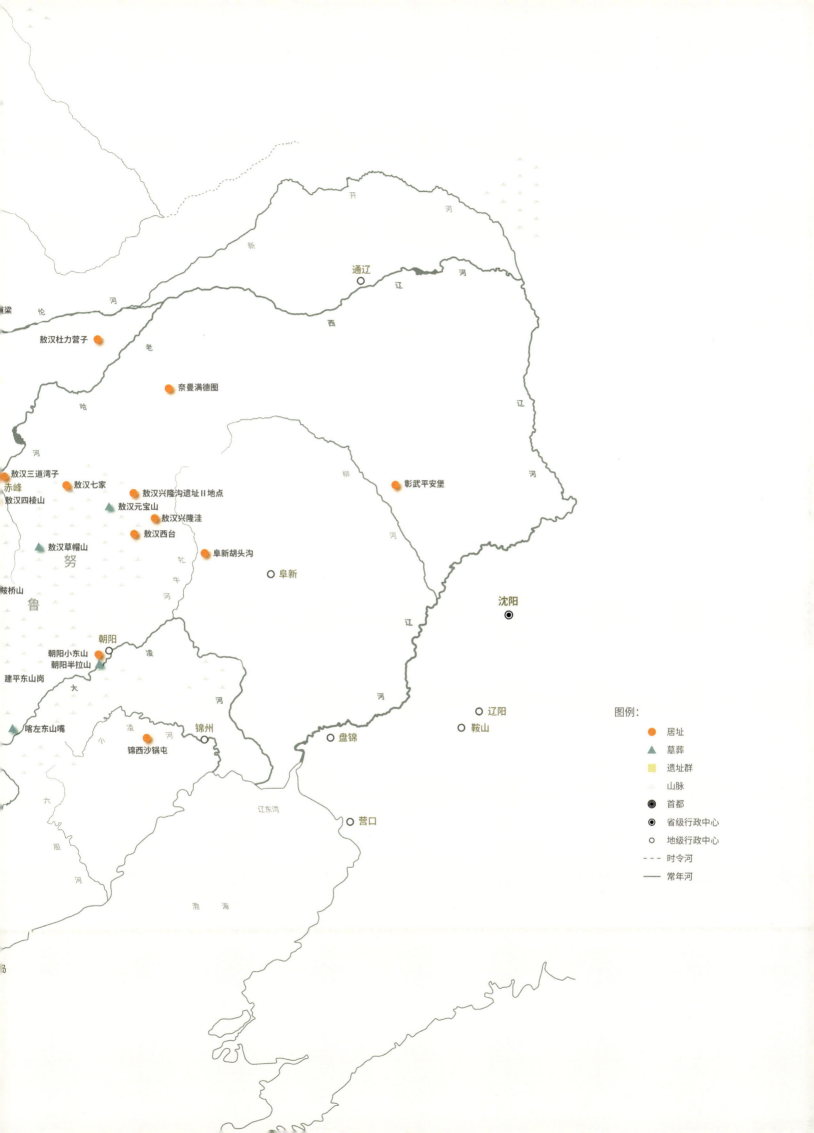

敖汉杜力营子 ●

奈曼满德图 ●

敖汉三道湾子 ●
赤峰
敖汉四棱山 ●
敖汉七家 ●
敖汉兴隆沟遗址Ⅱ地点 ●
敖汉元宝山 ▲
敖汉兴隆洼 ●
敖汉西台 ●
敖汉草帽山 ▲
努
阜新胡头沟 ●
阜新 ○

鞍桥山
鲁
朝阳
朝阳小东山
朝阳半拉山 ▲
建平东山岗

喀左东山嘴 ▲

锦西沙锅屯 ●
锦州 ○

通辽 ○

彰武平安堡 ●

沈阳 ◎

辽阳 ○
鞍山 ○
盘锦 ○

营口 ○

图例：

● 居址

▲ 墓葬

▢ 遗址群

山脉

◎ 首都

◉ 省级行政中心

○ 地级行政中心

--- 时令河

—— 常年河

引 言

　　红山后遗址，位于内蒙古自治区赤峰市红山，是红山文化重要的发现地，也是红山文化的命名地。

　　红山文化是距今约6500—5000年中国北方重要的新石器时代考古学文化，分布于辽宁省西部、内蒙古自治区东南部以及河北省北部地区，面积约二十万平方公里。

　　红山文化发展到距今约5500年左右，出现了以"坛、庙、冢"为代表的礼制建筑，形成了以玉龙为代表的玉礼器系统，进入到精神信仰体系化和社会结构复杂化阶段，成为中国最早迈入古国文明的代表性考古学文化，是中华文明的重要源头之一，被誉为中华文化的"直根系"。

　　红山文化古国文明考古成果，实证了中华文明延绵不绝、多元一体、兼收并蓄的总体特征，成为中国古代史的重要篇章，是需要我们弘扬和传承的历史文化遗产。

Introduction

Located at Hongshan ("red mountain") in Chifeng City, Inner Mongolia Autonomous Region, the Hongshanhou site is a significant discovery site of the Hongshan Culture and the place after which the culture is named.

The Hongshan Culture is an important Neolithic archaeological culture in northern China, dating back to approximately 6,500 to 5,000 years ago. It covers an area of about 200,000 square kilometers, including today's western Liaoning Province, southeastern Inner Mongolia Autonomous Region, and northern Hebei Province.

Around 5,500 years ago, the culture developed a ritual structure represented by "altars, temples, and burial mounds" and a jade ritual system symbolized by the jade dragon, entering a phase of the sophistication of social structure and the institutionalization of spirit and beliefs. As an archaeological culture, it represents the very first ancient state in China. As one of the important sources of Chinese civilization, it is hailed as the "taproot system" of Chinese culture.

The archaeological discoveries at the ancient state of the Hongshan Culture bear strong testimony to the fact that Chinese civilization is a highly inclusive continuum with a distinct identity. Serving as an amazing canto in the epic of ancient Chinese history, they are a cultural heritage worthy of our protection and promotion.

龙出辽河　The Dragon Emerges from the Liao River

　　红山文化兴起于西辽河流域，地处衔接东北平原、华北平原和蒙古高原的三角地带。距今约8000—5000年，辽河流域气候暖湿、环境适宜，温带森林与草原交接，成为东北渔猎文化与中原农耕文化交汇的前沿地带。特殊的自然和人文环境塑造了红山社会以渔猎为本、农业逐步发展的经济形态。红山文化大量继承了本地区文化传统，吸收了来自东北地区与中原地区文化因素，交流融合，兼收并蓄，形成了地域特征鲜明的文化特色，推动了红山社会的复杂化进程。

　　The Hongshan Culture emerged in the West Liao River basin, a triangular region connecting the Northeast Plain, the North China Plain, and the Mongolian Plateau. Between 8,000 and 5,000 years ago, the basin featured a warm and humid climate, with temperate forests meeting grasslands. This region became a frontier where the fishing and hunting culture of the Northeast intersected with the agricultural culture of the Central Plains. The particular natural and cultural environment shaped Hongshan society's economy, which was based on fishing and hunting, with agriculture gradually developing. It extensively inherited local traditions and absorbed diverse influences from both the Northeast and the Central Plains. This process, marked by strong inclusiveness, led to the formation of a distinctive cultural identity with salient regional characteristics and accelerated the sophistication of Hongshan society.

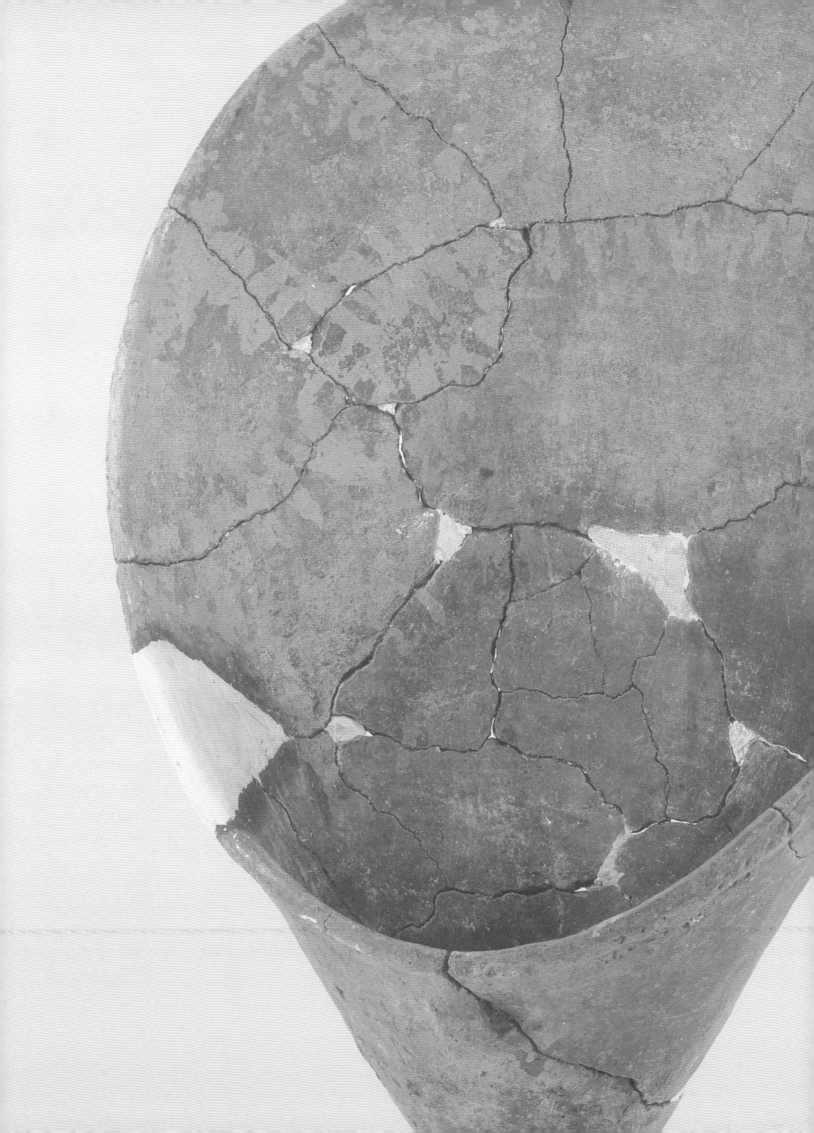

01

龙兴 Rise

西辽河流域有近万年的文化史，先后孕育了小河西文化、兴隆洼文化、赵宝沟文化、富河文化、红山文化、小河沿文化等。红山文化时期，生产力水平显著提升，以种植粟和黍为代表的旱作农业逐渐占据重要地位，聚落数量和规模远超以往。早期的红山文化吸收了本地区文化传统，继承和发展了以筒形陶罐为代表的器物类型和以压印"之"字纹为代表的纹饰系统，延续了以自然和生物崇拜为重要内容的信仰体系，并将龙崇拜推向成熟。

The West Liao River basin boasts a cultural history spanning nearly ten thousand years. It successively gave birth to the Xiaohexi, Xinglongwa, Zhaobaogou, Fuhe, Hongshan, and Xiaoheyan cultures. During the Hongshan Culture period, there was a significant increase in productivity. Dryland farming, primarily involving the cultivation of millet and broomcorn millet, gradually became influential. The number and scale of settlements far exceeded those of the previous periods. The early part of the culture absorbed local traditions, continuing and developing the typology of utensils represented by the cylindrical pottery jar and the system of decorations represented by the impressed zigzag pattern. It sustained a belief system that prominently featured the worship of nature and creatures, bringing dragon worship to maturity.

龙 出 辽 河

The Dragon Emerges
from the Liao River

『何以中国』文物考古大展系列

"The Essence of China," an Exhibition Series
of Cultural Relics and Archaeological Achievements

1. 龙纹陶片

兴隆洼文化（距今约 8000-7000 年）

1986-1994 年辽宁省阜新市查海遗址 23 号房址出土

F23:26 残长 6.5 厘米，宽 5.0 厘米

F23:27 残长 6.5 厘米，宽 3.5 厘米

辽宁省文物考古研究院藏

Pottery Shards with Dragon Pattern

Xinglongwa Culture (ca. 8,000–7,000 BP)

Unearthed from House Remains No. 23, Chahai Site, Fuxin, Liaoning between 1986 and 1994

F23:26: length (remaining) 6.5 cm, width 5.0 cm

F23:27: length (remaining) 6.5 cm, width 3.5 cm

Liaoning Provincial Institute of Cultural Relics and Archaeology

皆夹砂红褐陶，贴塑泥条，饰窝点纹为鳞。一件身直、尾部翘卷，似行龙；另一件身尾团卷，似蟠龙。

031

龙 出 辽 河
The Dragon Emerges
from the Liao River

龙腾中国：红山文化古国文明
Legends of Dragon：
The Ancient Civilization of Hongshan Culture

2. 鹿纹陶尊

赵宝沟文化（距今约 7200-6500 年）

1983 年内蒙古自治区赤峰市敖汉旗南台地遗址出土
高 20.2 厘米，口径 19.1 厘米，底径 10.5 厘米
内蒙古博物院藏

Pottery *Zun* (wine vessel) with Deer Pattern

Zhaobaogou Culture (ca. 7,200–6,500 BP)

Unearthed from the Nantaidi Site, Aohan Banner, Chifeng, Inner Mongolia in 1983

Height 20.2 cm, diameter of rim 19.1 cm, diameter of base 10.5 cm

Inner Mongolia Museum

龙 出 辽 河
The Dragon Emerges
from the Liao River

『何以中国』文物考古大展系列
"The Essence of China," an Exhibition Series
of Cultural Relics and Archaeological Achievements

　　夹细砂灰褐陶，器表和内壁都经过磨光处理。腹部压画两个鹿首神兽纹，鹿纹压出外形轮廓线，内压画细网格纹，网格均匀细密，间距只有一毫米左右。两鹿一长一短，有远近的透视效果。鹿身躯弯曲，生翼，目为柳叶形，尾部出半环加长三角形射线式纹。长体，鹿身起鳞。该器物制作精细，造型美观，绝非一般的生活用具，很可能是祭祀用的神器。

　　尊形器为赵宝沟文化燕北类型的一大特征器物。特别是饰有神化了的鹿首或者鹿首、鸟首结合等纹饰的尊形器，成为该文化的一大突出特征。南台地遗址中复原了 9 件尊形器，4 件饰有鹿首神兽等纹饰，其余饰以有编织特征的几何纹。

　　鹿纹装饰在赵宝沟文化遗址的器物上有不少发现，除尊形器外，还有豆、钵等器也装饰有鹿纹，而鹿纹在同时期周围其他文化中尚未发现。所以在赵宝沟文化中，鹿应该是人们日常生活中的重要伙伴，神化的鹿形象表现了赵宝沟文化先民对鹿的尊敬，也有可能是部落图腾。

3. 玦形石龙

左家山下层文化（距今约 7000—6000 年）

1985 年吉林省长春市农安县左家山遗址出土（T4 ② :1）
长 4.1 厘米，宽 3.9 厘米，厚 1.4 厘米，大孔径 1.0 厘米
中国国家博物馆藏

Stone Dragon in the Shape of *Jue* (slit ring)

Culture of the Lower Level of Zuojiashan (ca. 7,000–6,000 BP)

Unearthed from the Zuojiashan Site, Nong'an, Changchun, Jilin in 1985 (T4 ② :1)

Length 4.1 cm, width 3.9 cm, thickness 1.4 cm, diameter of bigger hole 1.0 cm

National Museum of China

034

龙 出 辽 河
The Dragon Emerges
from the Liao River

『何以中国』文物考古大展系列
"The Essence of China," an Exhibition Series
of Cultural Relics and Archaeological Achievements

　　灰白色霏细岩雕制。石龙周身光滑无纹，龙身蜷曲，首尾衔接呈玦形，衔接处雕出未断开的缺口，龙首部雕出双耳、吻部等轮廓，背部一穿孔，用于系挂。根据石龙出土地层信息，结合红山文化玦形玉龙从"首尾开口较小、内侧连接"向"首尾开口较大、不相连接"形态演变特点，此件石龙年代略早。

4. 筒形陶罐

兴隆洼文化（距今约 8000-7000 年）

1986-1994 年辽宁省阜新市查海遗址 46 号房址出土（F46：38）

高 23.8 厘米，口径 19.0 厘米，底径 11.2 厘米

辽宁省文物考古研究院藏

Cylindrical Pottery Jar

Xinglongwa Culture (ca. 8,000–7,000 BP)

Unearthed from House Remains No. 46, Chahai Site, Fuxin, Liaoning between 1986 and 1994 (F46:38)

Height 23.8 cm, diameter of rim 19.0 cm, diameter of base 11.2 cm

Liaoning Provincial Institute of Cultural Relics and Archaeology

夹砂黄褐陶，近口部泛黑，敞口，尖圆唇，斜直腹，平底。颈饰横压竖排"之"字纹，腹饰竖压横排"之"字纹。

5. 几何纹陶罐

赵宝沟文化（距今约 7200-6500 年）

内蒙古自治区赤峰市敖汉旗赵宝沟遗址出土
高 29.8 厘米，口径 26.7 厘米，底径 13.2 厘米
赤峰博物院藏

Jar with Geometric Pattern

Zhaobaogou Culture (ca. 7,200–6,500 BP)

Unearthed from the Zhaobaogou Site, Aohan Banner, Chifeng, Inner Mongolia

Height 29.8 cm, diameter of rim 26.7 cm, diameter of base 13.2 cm

Chifeng Museum

夹砂灰褐陶，平底，器身施满几何纹，口沿及器身有部分石膏修复。赵宝沟文化陶器上的几何纹是继素面陶器之后出现的比较早的陶器装饰纹，是新石器时代陶器上常见的一种纹饰。这种几何纹饰比较简单，主要源于生活的写实。

赵宝沟文化几何纹饰对后来红山文化及小河沿文化陶器上比较抽象化的几何纹装饰都有深远的影响。

037

龙 出 辽 河
The Dragon Emerges
from the Liao River

龙腾中国：红山文化古国文明
Legends of Dragon：
The Ancient Civilization of Hongshan Culture

6. 石器一组　Stone Artifacts

刮削器

红山文化（距今约 6500-5000 年）

2021 年辽宁省朝阳市建平县马鞍桥山遗址 50 号灰坑出土（H50∶9）

长 6.3 厘米，宽 1.3 厘米，厚 0.1 厘米

辽宁省文物考古研究院藏

Scraper

Hongshan Culture (ca. 6,500–5,000 BP)

Unearthed from Ash Pit No. 50, Mount Ma'anqiao Site, Jianping, Chaoyang, Liaoning in 2021 (H50:9)

Length 6.3 cm, width 1.3 cm, thickness 0.1 cm

Liaoning Provincial Institute of Cultural Relics and Archaeology

038

龙 出 辽 河
The Dragon Emerges
from the Liao River

『何以中国』文物考古大展系列
"The Essence of China:" an Exhibition Series
of Cultural Relics and Archaeological Achievements

完整。玛瑙石。白色，长条状。单面直刃。

石核

红山文化（距今约 6500-5000 年）

2023 年辽宁省朝阳市建平县马鞍桥山遗址 3 号沟出土（G3∶3）

长 3.5 厘米，宽 2.0 厘米，厚 1.4 厘米

辽宁省文物考古研究院藏

Lithic Core

Hongshan Culture (ca. 6,500–5,000 BP)

Unearthed from Ditch No. 3, Mount Ma'anqiao Site, Jianping, Chaoyang, Liaoning in 2023 (G3:3)

Length 3.5 cm, width 2.0 cm, thickness 1.4 cm

Liaoning Provincial Institute of Cultural Relics and Archaeology

完整。燧石。紫褐色。圆锥体。

石镞

红山文化（距今约 6500-5000 年）

2021-2022 年辽宁省朝阳市建平县马鞍桥山遗址出土或采集（T0357 ① :1，H62:11，H73:2，采集）

长 3.5 厘米，宽 1.2 厘米

长 2.8 厘米，宽 1.1 厘米

长 2.1 厘米，宽 1.2 厘米

长 2.0 厘米，宽 1.5 厘米

辽宁省文物考古研究院藏

Stone Arrowheads

Hongshan Culture (ca. 6,500–5,000 BP)

Unearthed or collected from the Mount Ma'anqiao Site, Jianping, Chaoyang,

Liaoning between 2021 and 2022 (T0357 ① :1, H62:11, H73:2)

Length 3.5 cm, width 1.2 cm

Length 2.8 cm, width 1.1 cm

Length 2.1 cm, width 1.2 cm

Length 2.0 cm, width 1.5 cm

Liaoning Provincial Institute of Cultural Relics and Archaeology

039

龙 出 辽 河
The Dragon Emerges
from the Liao River

龙腾中国：红山文化古国文明
Legends of Dragon：
The Ancient Civilization of Hongshan Culture

　　均完整。三件为燧石，红色。一件为玛瑙，白色。体轻薄，通体压制。平面呈圆角三角形或圆叶形。

7. 穿孔石饰件

红山文化（距今约 6500-5000 年）

2021 年辽宁省朝阳市建平县马鞍桥山遗址出土（T0757 ② :19）

高 8.0 厘米，宽 4.3 厘米，厚 0.9 厘米

辽宁省文物考古研究院藏

Perforated Stone Ornament

Hongshan Culture (ca. 6,500–5,000 BP)

Unearthed from the Mount Ma'anqiao Site, Jianping, Chaoyang, Liaoning in 2021 (T0757 ② :19)

Height 8.0 cm, width 4.3 cm, thickness 0.9 cm

Liaoning Provincial Institute of Cultural Relics and Archaeology

龙出辽河
The Dragon Emerges
from the Liao River

「何以中国」文物考古大展系列
"The Essence of China," an Exhibition Series
of Cultural Relics and Archaeological Achievements

灰白色。体扁平、厚重，通体磨制，形制规整。上部平面近圆形，近顶部中间位置对钻一孔，下部呈长方形，底端窄小，呈斜面。

8. 双耳折腹陶罐

红山文化（距今约 6500-5000 年）

2019 年辽宁省朝阳市建平县马鞍桥山遗址 8 号房址出土（F8：2）

高 16.6 厘米，口径 15.3 厘米，底径 8.9 厘米

辽宁省文物考古研究院藏

Double-handled Pottery Jar with a Folded Belly

Hongshan Culture (ca. 6,500–5,000 BP)

Unearthed from House Remains No.8, Mount Ma'anqiao Site, Jianping, Chaoyang, Liaoning in 2019

Height 16.6 cm, diameter of rim 15.3 cm, diameter of base 8.9 cm

Liaoning Provincial Institute of Cultural Relics and Archaeology

041

龙 出 辽 河
The Dragon Emerges
from the Liao River

龙腾中国：红山文化古国文明
Legends of Dragon：
The Ancient Civilization of Hongshan Culture

夹砂黑陶。敛口，圆唇，圆肩。肩部对称饰两个素面长条形竖桥状耳。器体内、外壁通体磨光。肩部饰一周戳刺短平行线纹，上腹部饰折线勾连纹，纹饰由六组"之"字形图案相互勾连构成，每组"之"字形图案由二或三道复线"之"字组成。底部饰席纹。

9. 涂朱石耜

红山文化（距今约 6500-5000 年）

2022 年辽宁省朝阳市建平县马鞍桥山遗址 1 号祭祀坑出土（JK1:29）

高 24.0 厘米，宽 11.0 厘米，厚 1.5 厘米

辽宁省文物考古研究院藏

Red-painted Stone *Si* (farm tool)

Hongshan Culture (ca. 6,500–5,000 BP)

Unearthed from Sacrificial Pit No. 1, Mount Ma'anqiao Site, Jianping, Chaoyang, Liaoning in 2022 (JK1:29)

Height 24.0 cm, width 11.0 cm, thickness 1.5 cm

Liaoning Provincial Institute of Cultural Relics and Archaeology

龙 出 辽 河

The Dragon Emerges
from the Liao River

『何以中国』文物考古大展系列

"The Essence of China," an Exhibition Series
of Cultural Relics and Archaeological Achievements

　　青绿色石质。通体磨制兼打制。器体扁平、宽大、厚重，体表磨制光滑。柄部两侧为双面打制，呈束腰状，柄端打制成圆弧状。尖部也为圆弧状，磨制光滑，双面弧刃。体表两侧饰红色彩绘，图案不详。

10. 石磨盘及石磨棒

红山文化（距今约 6500-5000 年）

2022 年辽宁省朝阳市建平县马鞍桥山遗址 1 号祭祀坑出土（JK1:31，JK1:32）

石磨盘通长 41.0 厘米，宽 26.1 厘米，厚 5.8 厘米

石磨棒通长 32.3 厘米，宽 8.1 厘米，厚 3.9 厘米

辽宁省文物考古研究院藏

Millstone and Stone Grinding Roller

Hongshan Culture (ca. 6,500–5,000 BP)

Unearthed from Sacrificial Pit No. 1, Mount Ma'anqiao Site, Jianping, Chaoyang, Liaoning in 2022 (JK1:31, JK1:32)

Millstone: overall length 41.0 cm, width 26.1 cm, thickness 5.8 cm

Stone grinding roller: overall length 32.3 cm, width 8.1 cm, thickness 3.9 cm

Liaoning Provincial Institute of Cultural Relics and Archaeology

　　黄褐色砂岩。器体形制规整。石磨盘平面呈圆角长方形，体宽大、厚重。底面和四周边缘均为打制，布满细小疤痕。单面使用，磨面磨损较严重，内凹明显，呈两端高、中间低。石磨棒呈扁长条状体，中间较宽厚，两端略细薄。单面使用，磨面较平滑。

龙 出 辽 河
The Dragon Emerges
from the Liao River

『何以中国』文物考古大展系列
"The Essence of China," an Exhibition Series
of Cultural Relics and Archaeological Achievements

11. 石斧

红山文化（距今约 6500-5000 年）

2022 年辽宁省朝阳市建平县马鞍桥山遗址 1 号祭祀坑出土（JK1:25）

通长 12.0 厘米，宽 7.0 厘米，厚 2.3 厘米

辽宁省文物考古研究院藏

Stone Axe

Hongshan Culture (ca. 6,500–5,000 BP)

Unearthed from Sacrificial Pit No. 1, Mount Ma'anqiao Site, Jianping, Chaoyang, Liaoning in 2022 (JK1:25)

Overall length 12.0 cm, width 7.0 cm, thickness 2.3 cm

Liaoning Provincial Institute of Cultural Relics and Archaeology

　　青灰色石质。通体磨制光滑，平面呈圆角梯形。弧顶。圆弧刃，双面磨制，刃部布满细小的使用疤痕。

12. 石刀

红山文化（距今约 6500-5000 年）

2022 年辽宁省朝阳市建平县马鞍桥山遗址 1 号祭祀坑出土（JK1：44）

通长 12.0 厘米，宽 3.5 厘米，厚 0.3 厘米

辽宁省文物考古研究院藏

Stone Knife

Hongshan Culture (ca. 6,500–5,000 BP)

Unearthed from Sacrificial Pit No. 1, Mount Ma'anqiao Site, Jianping, Chaoyang, Liaoning in 2022 (JK1:44)

Overall length 12.0 cm, width 3.5 cm, thickness 0.3 cm

Liaoning Provincial Institute of Cultural Relics and Archaeology

青灰色叶岩。体扁平、细长，呈椭圆形，通体磨制光滑。弧背，背部中间对穿两孔。直刃，刃部锋利。

龙 出 辽 河
The Dragon Emerges
from the Liao River

龙腾中国：红山文化古国文明
Legends of Dragon：
The Ancient Civilization of Hongshan Culture

13. 陶斜口器

红山文化（距今约 6500-5000 年）

2022 年辽宁省朝阳市建平县马鞍桥山遗址 1 号祭祀坑出土（JK1：22）

通高 47.0 厘米，宽 36.0 厘米，底径 9.1 厘米

辽宁省文物考古研究院藏

Pottery Vessel with an Oblique Rim

Hongshan Culture (ca. 6,500–5,000 BP)

Unearthed from Sacrificial Pit No. 1, Mount Ma'anqiao Site, Jianping, Chaoyang, Liaoning in 2022 (JK1:22)

Overall height 47.0 cm, width 36.0 cm, diameter of base 9.1 cm

Liaoning Provincial Institute of Cultural Relics and Archaeology

夹砂黄褐陶。色泽不均匀，器表呈黄褐色，内壁下部为黑褐色。造型似簸箕状。前沿低矮外侈，圆唇。前沿下有一横錾耳，呈半圆形，扁平起棱。两侧口沿呈弧形。背沿与前沿高度上下相差悬殊，背沿尖方唇，背面器壁斜直外侈。小平底。

龙 出 辽 河
The Dragon Emerges
from the Liao River

『何 以 中 国』文 物 考 古 大 展 系 列
"The Essence of China," an Exhibition Series
of Cultural Relics and Archaeological Achievements

14. 彩陶双耳罐

红山文化（距今约 6500-5000 年）

2021 年辽宁省朝阳市建平县马鞍桥山遗址 1 号祭祀坑出土（JK1:16）

高 14.5 厘米，口径 14.5 厘米，底径 8.0 厘米

辽宁省文物考古研究院藏

Double-handled Painted Pottery Jar

Hongshan Culture (ca. 6,500–5,000 BP)

Unearthed from Sacrificial Pit No. 1, Mount Ma'anqiao Site, Jianping, Chaoyang, Liaoning in 2021 (JK1:16)

Height 14.5 cm, diameter of rim 14.5 cm, diameter of base 8.0 cm

Liaoning Provincial Institute of Cultural Relics and Archaeology

泥质红陶。直口，圆唇，折肩，深弧腹，小平底。双竖桥耳置于上腹部。器表上部饰黑彩斜线纹，下部饰黑彩勾连涡纹。

龙 出 辽 河
The Dragon Emerges
from the Liao River

『何以中国』文物考古大展系列
"The Essence of China." an Exhibition Series
of Cultural Relics and Archaeological Achievements

15. 彩陶双耳罐

红山文化（距今约 6500-5000 年）

2022 年辽宁省朝阳市建平县马鞍桥山遗址 1 号祭祀坑出土（JK1:1）

高 48.0 厘米，口径 22.0 厘米，底径 10.0 厘米

辽宁省文物考古研究院藏

Double-handled Painted Pottery Jar

Hongshan Culture (ca. 6,500–5,000 BP)

Unearthed from Sacrificial Pit No. 1, Mount Ma'anqiao Site, Jianping, Chaoyang, Liaoning in 2022 (JK1:1)

Height 48.0 cm, diameter of rim 22.0 cm, diameter of base 10.0 cm

Liaoning Provincial Institute of Cultural Relics and Archaeology

泥质红陶。折沿，圆唇，溜肩，鼓腹，器形瘦高，小平底，桥形双耳置于中腹下。饰黑彩涡纹。

龙 出 辽 河
The Dragon Emerges
from the Liao River

龙腾中国：红山文化古国文明
Legends of Dragon：
The Ancient Civilization of Hongshan Culture

融合 Integration

龙 出 辽 河
The Dragon Emerges
from the Liao River

『何以中国』文物考古大展系列
"The Essence of China," an Exhibition Series
of Cultural Relics and Archaeological Achievements

　　红山文化与周边考古学文化保持着长期交流关系。对周边文化因素的吸收与利用，促进了文化发展，扩展了陶器种类，丰富了器物制作和表现方式。圜底釜、器座和彩陶的器物造型、制作技术均源自黄河流域，最终被红山文化吸收，成为文化交流的典型例证。红山文化中显示了南北文化交流，不同文化因素共存共融，孕育出新技术与新观念，为红山社会增添了新的活力。

The Hongshan Culture maintained long-term interactions and exchanges with surrounding archaeological cultures. Its development was facilitated by its absorption and utilization of elements from these neighbors. This led to a noticeable increase in pottery types, enriching the methods of artifact manufacture and design. The shapes and production techniques of round-bottomed pots, vessel stands, and painted pottery had all originated from the Yellow River basin and were eventually integrated into the Hongshan Culture, becoming exemplary evidence of cultural exchanges: a north-south interaction, where different elements coexisted and merged, gave birth to new crafts and concepts and thus infused the Hongshan society with more vitality.

16. "之"字纹筒形陶罐

红山文化（距今约 6500-5000 年）

2008 年内蒙古自治区赤峰市魏家窝铺遗址 11 号灰坑出土

高 21.0 厘米，口径 23.1 厘米，底径 8.4 厘米

内蒙古自治区文物考古研究院藏

Cylindrical Pottery Jar with Zigzag Pattern

Hongshan Culture (ca. 6,500–5,000 BP)

Unearthed from Ash Pit No. 11, Weijiawopu Site, Chifeng, Inner Mongolia in 2008

Height 21.0 cm, diameter of rim 23.1 cm, diameter of base 8.4 cm

Inner Mongolia Institute of Cultural Relics and Archaeology

夹砂陶，侈口，筒形腹，平底。器身纹饰为"之"字纹，口沿较直，腹部呈筒状，较为规整。

051

龙 出 辽 河
The Dragon Emerges
from the Liao River

龙腾中国：红山文化古国文明
Legends of Dragon：
The Ancient Civilization of Hongshan Culture

17. 彩陶钵

红山文化（距今约 6500-5000 年）

2008 年内蒙古自治区赤峰市魏家窝铺遗址 4 号沟出土

高 10.0 厘米，口径 14.5 厘米，底径 5.0 厘米

内蒙古自治区文物考古研究院藏

Painted Pottery *Bo* (food vessel)

Hongshan Culture (ca. 6,500–5,000 BP)

Unearthed from Ditch No. 4, Weijiawopu Site, Chifeng, Inner Mongolia in 2008

Height 10.0 cm, diameter of rim 14.5 cm, diameter of base 5.0 cm

Inner Mongolia Institute of Cultural Relics and Archaeology

龙 出 辽 河
The Dragon Emerges
from the Liao River
——
『何以中国』文物考古大展系列
"The Essence of China," an Exhibition Series
of Cultural Relics and Archaeological Achievements

红陶。敞口、弧腹、圜底。主体底色接近灰白色，带有彩绘纹饰。上有平行的线条纹。

18. 红陶钵及器座

红山文化（距今约 6500-5000 年）

2019 年辽宁省朝阳市建平县马鞍桥山遗址 25 号灰坑出土（H25：8）

通高 19.0 厘米

辽宁省文物考古研究院藏

Red Pottery *Bo* (food vessel) and Its Stand

Hongshan Culture (ca. 6,500–5,000 BP)

Unearthed from Ash Pit No.25, Mount Ma'anqiao Site, Jianping, Chaoyang, Liaoning in 2019

Overall height 19.0 cm

Liaoning Provincial Institute of Cultural Relics and Archaeology

053

龙 出 辽 河
The Dragon Emerges
from the Liao River

龙腾中国：红山文化古国文明
Legends of Dragon：
The Ancient Civilization of Hongshan Culture

　　泥质红陶，素面，饰红陶衣，无彩。陶钵敛口，圆唇，口沿外壁加厚。弧腹，小平底。器座上口细、底口粗，呈喇叭形，上口沿外折，底口近平沿，底沿外侧起台。

19. 彩陶器座

红山文化（距今约 6500-5000 年）

2021 年辽宁省朝阳市建平县马鞍桥山遗址 61 号灰坑出土（H61：3）

高 14.0 厘米，口径 19.0 厘米，底径 21.0 厘米

辽宁省文物考古研究院藏

Stand of a Painted Pottery Vessel

Hongshan Culture (ca. 6,500–5,000 BP)

Unearthed from Ash Pit No. 61, Mount Ma'anqiao Site, Jianping, Chaoyang, Liaoning in 2021 (H61:3)

Height 14.0 cm, diameter of rim 19.0 cm, diameter of base 21.0 cm

Liaoning Provincial Institute of Cultural Relics and Archaeology

054

龙 出 辽 河
The Dragon Emerges
from the Liao River

『何以中国』文物考古大展系列
"The Essence of China." an Exhibition Series
of Cultural Relics and Archaeological Achievements

　　泥质红陶。器体上口细、底口粗，呈喇叭形，上口沿外折，底口近平沿，底沿外侧起台。器表有一层红陶衣，色泽匀称，其上饰黑彩条形纹。

20. 彩陶双耳壶

红山文化（距今约 6500-5000 年）

2021 年辽宁省朝阳市建平县马鞍桥山遗址 47 号灰坑出土（H47:2）

高 14.0 厘米，口径 7.5 厘米，底径 7.0 厘米

辽宁省文物考古研究院藏

Double-handled Painted Pottery Pot

Hongshan Culture (ca. 6,500–5,000 BP)

Unearthed from Ash Pit No. 47, Mount Ma'anqiao Site, Jianping, Chaoyang, Liaoning in 2021 (H47:2)

Height 14.0 cm, diameter of rim 7.5 cm, diameter of base 7.0 cm

Liaoning Provincial Institute of Cultural Relics and Archaeology

　　泥质红陶。敞口，圆唇，弧腹。双桥耳置于上腹部，肩部饰一周竖向平行线纹，黑彩，下部饰黑彩勾连涡纹。另外在下腹部有两个孔，底部中间有一个孔，经推测均为人有意敲打而成，应具有特殊含义。

21. 彩陶尊

红山文化（距今约 6500-5000 年）

内蒙古自治区赤峰市翁牛特旗敖汉营子遗址采集

高 44.0 厘米，口径 16.0 厘米，腹径 26.0 厘米，底径 9.7 厘米

翁牛特旗博物馆（翁牛特旗文物保护中心）藏

Painted Pottery *Zun* (wine vessel)

Hongshan Culture (ca. 6,500–5,000 BP)

Found at the Aohanyingzi Site, Ongniud Banner, Chifeng, Inner Mongolia

Height 44.0 cm, diameter of rim 16.0 cm, diameter of belly 26.0 cm, diameter of base 9.7 cm

Ongniud Museum (Ongniud Banner Conservation Center of Cultural Relics)

泥质红陶，口微敛，圆唇，粗颈，深腹近底部稍鼓，小平底。口至腹中部间用黑彩绘对称的四组图案，每组以一竖条为中心，自里向外绘三条同心垂弧纹，图案优美简洁。

龙 出 辽 河
The Dragon Emerges
from the Liao River

『何以中国』文物考古大展系列
"The Essence of China," an Exhibition Series
of Cultural Relics and Archaeological Achievements

22. 彩陶双耳罐

红山文化（距今约 6500-5000 年）

内蒙古自治区赤峰市敖汉旗新惠镇出土

残高 11.7 厘米，口径 5.2 厘米，腹径 21.5 厘米，底径 9.6 厘米

赤峰博物院藏

Double-handled Painted Pottery Jar

Hongshan Culture (ca. 6,500–5,000 BP)

Unearthed from Xinhui Town, Aohan Banner, Chifeng, Inner Mongolia

Height (remaining) 11.7 cm, diameter of rim 5.2 cm, diameter of belly 21.5 cm, diameter of base 9.6 cm

Chifeng Museum

泥质磨光红陶。小口，圆肩，圆腹，下腹内收，平底。上腹壁两侧捏塑环形耳，肩部饰放射状黑色线条，线条之间饰一周鳞纹，下腹部饰勾连纹。

23. 彩陶筒形罐

红山文化（距今约 6500-5000 年）

1974 年内蒙古自治区赤峰市阿鲁科尔沁旗巴彦塔拉苏木出土
高 35.2 厘米，口径 27.0 厘米，腹径 24.0 厘米，底径 12.2 厘米
阿鲁科尔沁旗博物馆藏

Cylindrical Painted Pottery Jar

Hongshan Culture (ca. 6,500–5,000 BP)

Unearthed from Bayantala Sum, Ar Horqin Banner, Chifeng, Inner Mongolia in 1974
Height 35.2 cm, diameter of rim 27.0 cm, diameter of belly 24.0 cm, diameter of base 12.2 cm
Ar Horqin Banner Museum

龙 出 辽 河
The Dragon Emerges
from the Liao River

『何以中国』文物考古大展系列
"The Essence of China," an Exhibition Series
of Cultural Relics and Archaeological Achievements

　　侈口、筒形腹、平底，红陶质地、外绘黑彩，肩有两小突起。该陶罐汇聚中亚的菱形方格纹、仰韶文化的玫瑰花纹及红山文化的龙鳞纹，印证了五千年前亚洲东西和中国南北几种古文化在辽西地区的交流融汇。

24. 彩陶钵

红山文化（距今约 6500-5000 年）

高 10.6 厘米，口径 21.3-21.8 厘米，腹径 22.0 厘米

朝阳博物馆藏

Painted Pottery *Bo* (food vessel)

Hongshan Culture (ca. 6,500–5,000 BP)

Height 10.6 cm, diameter of rim 21.3–21.8 cm, diameter of belly 22.0 cm

Chaoyang Museum

059

龙 出 辽 河
The Dragon Emerges
from the Liao River

龙腾中国：红山文化古国文明
Legends of Dragon：
The Ancient Civilization of Hongshan Culture

　　泥质红陶，器体外着红色陶衣。侈口束颈，弧腹平底。口沿下至上腹部绘一周黑彩单勾旋纹，腹部绘一周勾连涡纹带。

　　红山文化祭祀用陶器主要为泥质红陶，且多为彩陶。红山文化彩陶受到中原地区仰韶文化的影响，在自身文化的发展中又融合了异质文化，体现红山先民的高容纳度和在自身发展中不断充实的历史过程。

龙行红山 The Dragon Flies along the Mountains

距今约5500年，红山文化进入晚期阶段，社会发展进一步加速，聚落等级和功能产生分化，出现了远离居址、不同规模的礼仪场所，形成了由神庙、祭坛、积石冢构成的祭祀体系，体现了以祭祖和祭天为主要内容的祭祀文化，标志着红山社会迈入文明阶段。大型礼仪中心牛河梁遗址群的规划、设计、营建，是红山古国生产力水平和文明成就的集中反映。

Around 5,500 years ago, the Hongshan Culture entered its late phase, with accelerated social development and differentiated settlement classes and functions. Ritual sites of various scales emerged, distant from residential areas. A sacrificial system comprising temples, altars, and stone burial mounds was established, reflecting a ritual culture primarily focused on ancestor and heaven worship, signifying the entry of Hongshan society into a civilized stage. The planning, design, and construction of the Niuheliang site complex as a large ritual center epitomize the productivity level and civilizational achievements of the ancient state of Hongshan.

01

崇祖 Worship of Ancestors

062

龙 行 红 山

The Dragon Flies along
the Mountains

『 何 以 中 国 』 文 物 考 古 大 展 系 列

"The Essence of China," an Exhibition Series
of Cultural Relics and Archaeological Achievements

　　祖先崇拜在西辽河流域有深厚的文化根基，是红山文化信仰体系的重要内容。红山先民将祖先作为偶像崇拜，所制人像材质多样、工艺精湛、大小有别，不仅出现在居住区的房址内，也供奉于神庙、祭坛等礼仪场所。位于牛河梁遗址第一地点的"女神庙"，坐落在规模宏大的人工堆砌台基之上，遗址中发现的大规模群像，为其他遗址所未见。"女神庙"的神像地位崇高，由红山社会共有，代表了红山先民共同崇拜的远祖。

　　Ancestor worship, deeply rooted in the West Liao River basin, was a vital component of the Hongshan Culture's belief system. The Hongshan people idolized their ancestors, making human figures of varying sizes from diverse materials with exquisite craftsmanship. These figures were not only found within residential areas but also venerated at ritual sites such as temples and altars. At locus No. 1 of the Niuheliang site, a Goddess Temple was built on a grand man-made platform. There large-scale group statues were discovered, which have not been found at other archaeological sites. The deity of the temple held an exalted status and was worshipped by the entire Hongshan society as its people's common distant progenitor.

25. 陶塔形器残件和底座

红山文化（距今约 6500-5000 年）

1989 年辽宁省朝阳市建平县牛河梁遗址第二地点四号冢 4 号墓出土

N2Z4M4:W60　残高 19.3 厘米，上径 10.0 厘米，下径 13.0 厘米

N2Z4M4:W57　残高 28.2 厘米，上口径 11.0 厘米，底径 51.4 厘米

辽宁省文物考古研究院藏

Fragment of a Pagoda-shaped Painted Pottery Vessel, Stand of a Pagoda-shaped Painted Pottery Vessel

Hongshan Culture (ca. 6,500–5,000 BP)

Unearthed from Tomb No. 4, Stone Mound No. 4, Locus No. 2, Niuheliang Site, Jianping, Chaoyang, Liaoning in 1989

N2Z4M4:W60: Height (remaining) 19.3 cm, upper diameter 10.0 cm, lower diameter 13.0 cm

N2Z4M4:W57: Height (remaining) 28.2 cm, diameter of upper rim 11.0 cm, diameter of base 51.4 cm

Liaoning Provincial Institute of Cultural Relics and Archaeology

一件似为塔形器的口部与上腹部残件。上部呈直筒状，筒的上下两端起一道横截面呈三角形的凸箍；下接的腹部外敞，上绘勾连纹黑彩。器表施红陶衣。

另一件为塔形器底座残件。覆钵状，底大口、内敛，短平沿，方圆唇，沿上有折起圆棱。座身由底向上呈外弧状内收，如倒置的陶盆，上部可见残断的束腰镂孔痕迹，从残断处保留两组镂孔的下孔缘分析，其上应为四等分的长方形镂孔与遗留的板状支隔。通体施红陶衣，绘黑彩勾连纹，纹样以无卷勾的弧线三角为基本单元，组成带状图案，从上到下共九道，各组由短渐长，相间均匀，近于满布全基座。

26. 彩陶塔形器

红山文化（距今约 6500-5000 年）

1996 年辽宁省朝阳市建平县牛河梁遗址第二地点二号冢出土（N2Z2:49）
残高 55.0 厘米，上腹径 18.0 厘米，束腰径 15.0 厘米，底径 44.6 厘米
辽宁省文物考古研究院藏

Pagoda-shaped Painted Pottery Vessel

Hongshan Culture (ca. 6,500–5,000 BP)

Unearthed from Stone Mound No. 2, Locus No. 2, Niuheliang Site, Jianping, Chaoyang, Liaoning in 1996 (N2Z2:49)

Height (remaining) 55.0 cm, diameter of upper belly 18.0 cm, diameter of narrow waist 15.0 cm, diameter of base 44.6 cm

Liaoning Provincial Institute of Cultural Relics and Archaeology

　　近于复原。泥质红陶，有红陶衣。双口，口
上端残缺，可见口下起一凸棱。颈部呈椭圆形，
颈筒壁下部并联，腹部较鼓，呈覆钵状，腹下部
内收，腹面满压窝点纹，再施挂黑彩。腹下出甚
宽的裙边，以与束腰相接。束腰以中部一方棱为
界分为上下两部分，上下各有镂孔 4 个，上部镂
孔近倒梯形，顶边外弧，下部镂孔为竖长方形。
方棱在与镂孔相间部位饰 4 个小泥饼，饼面压画
"十"字装饰。覆钵状底座，座面绘 4 组以平行
横线相间的黑彩勾连涡纹带。该器的残片多发现
于冢体北墙中段处，是此类器物唯一近于通体复
原的一件。

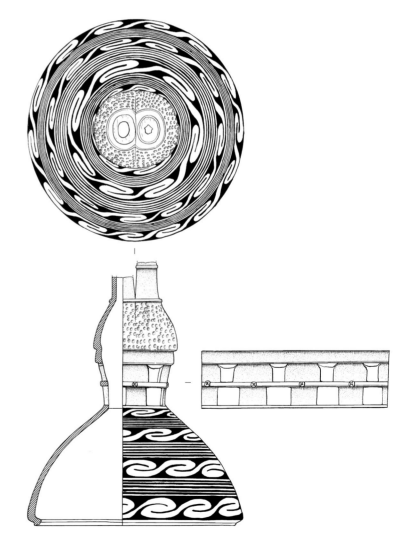

27. 陶器盖

红山文化（距今约 6500-5000 年）

1983-1985 年辽宁省朝阳市凌源市牛河梁遗址第一地点"女神庙"出土（N1J1B:10）

高 8.4 厘米，口径 11.7 厘米

辽宁省文物考古研究院藏

Pottery Vessel Lid

Hongshan Culture (ca. 6,500–5,000 BP)

Unearthed from the Goddess Temple, Locus No. 1, Niuheliang Site, Lingyuan, Chaoyang, Liaoning between 1983 and 1985 (N1J1B:10)

Height 8.4 cm, diameter of rim 11.7 cm

Liaoning Provincial Institute of Cultural Relics and Archaeology

　　泥质红陶。形如倒置的豆。柄呈喇叭状，盖的沿腹间起明显折棱。盖面饰篦点式压印"之"字纹 5 周，有镂孔四组间小泥饼 4 个，镂孔为长条状，每组 5 条。喇叭状柄口与柄体交接处和盖面与盖口交接处各饰一周附加锥刺纹。

28. 泥塑熊鼻残件

红山文化（距今约 6500-5000 年）

1983-1985 年辽宁省朝阳市凌源市牛河梁遗址第一地点"女神庙"出土（N1J1B:7）

高 10.0 厘米，残长 11.5 厘米，宽 8.0 厘米

辽宁省文物考古研究院藏

Clay Sculpture (incomplete) of a Bear's Nose

Hongshan Culture (ca. 6,500–5,000 BP)

Unearthed from the Goddess Temple, Locus No. 1, Niuheliang Site, Lingyuan, Chaoyang, Liaoning between 1983 and 1985 (N1J1B:7)

Height 10.0 cm, length (remaining) 11.5 cm, width 8.0 cm

Liaoning Provincial Institute of Cultural Relics and Archaeology

草拌泥质。圆吻端保存完整，甚匀称，稍显上翘，下有两鼻孔，呈椭圆形，再下为甚平的底面。

29. 泥塑熊下颌残件

红山文化（距今约 6500-5000 年）

1983-1985 年辽宁省朝阳市凌源市牛河梁遗址第一地点"女神庙"出土（N1J1A∶7）
辽宁省文物考古研究院藏

Clay Sculpture (incomplete) of a Bear's Lower Jaw

Hongshan Culture (ca. 6,500–5,000 BP)

Unearthed from the Goddess Temple, Locus No. 1, Niuheliang Site, Lingyuan, Chaoyang, Liaoning between 1983 and 1985 (N1J1A:7)
Liaoning Provincial Institute of Cultural Relics and Archaeology

草拌泥质。残件上有牙齿，獠牙较长，上涂白彩。

龙 行 红 山
The Dragon Flies along
the Mountains

『何以中国』文物考古大展系列
"The Essence of China," an Exhibition Series
of Cultural Relics and Archaeological Achievements

30. 泥塑熊爪残件

红山文化（距今约 6500-5000 年）

1983-1985 年辽宁省朝阳市凌源市牛河梁遗址第一地点"女神庙"出土（N1J1B:8-2）

高 7.5 厘米，长 14.5 厘米，宽 12.0 厘米

辽宁省文物考古研究院藏

Clay Sculpture (incomplete) of a Bear's Paw

Hongshan Culture (ca. 6,500–5,000 BP)

Unearthed from the Goddess Temple, Locus No. 1, Niuheliang Site, Lingyuan, Chaoyang, Liaoning between 1983 and 1985 (N1J1B:8-2)

Height 7.5 cm, length 14.5 cm, width 12.0 cm

Liaoning Provincial Institute of Cultural Relics and Archaeology

草拌泥质。显四趾，侧二趾短，关节隐现。

069

龙 行 红 山
The Dragon Flies along
the Mountains

龙腾中国：红山文化古国文明
Legends of Dragon :
The Ancient Civilization of Hongshan Culture

31. 泥塑翅膀残件

红山文化（距今约 6500-5000 年）

1983-1985 年辽宁省朝阳市凌源市牛河梁遗址第一地点"女神庙"出土（N1J1B:9-2）

残长 46.0 厘米，宽 24.0 厘米

辽宁省文物考古研究院藏

Clay Sculpture (incomplete) of a Wing

Hongshan Culture (ca. 6,500–5,000 BP)

Unearthed from the Goddess Temple, Locus No. 1, Niuheliang Site, Lingyuan, Chaoyang, Liaoning between 1983 and 1985 (N1J1B:9-2)

Length (remaining) 46.0 cm, width 24.0 cm

Liaoning Provincial Institute of Cultural Relics and Archaeology

龙 行 红 山
The Dragon Flies along
the Mountains

『何以中国』文物考古大展系列
"The Essence of China," an Exhibition Series
of Cultural Relics and Archaeological Achievements

草拌泥质。左侧与后部残缺。表面磨光。右翼保存较好，为三分翅，有中脊。

32. 泥塑鹰爪残件

红山文化（距今约 6500-5000 年）

1983-1985 年辽宁省朝阳市凌源市牛河梁遗址第一地点"女神庙"出土（N1J1B：9-1）

长 13.5 厘米、14.5 厘米

辽宁省文物考古研究院藏

Clay Sculptures (incomplete) of an Eagle's Claws

Hongshan Culture (ca. 6,500–5,000 BP)

Unearthed from the Goddess Temple, Locus No. 1, Niuheliang Site, Lingyuan, Chaoyang, Liaoning between 1983 and 1985 (N1J1B:9-1)

Length 13.5 cm and 14.5 cm

Liaoning Provincial Institute of Cultural Relics and Archaeology

草拌泥质。为两爪，均残，各存一侧二趾，趾弯曲并拢，每趾三节，关节突出，趾尖锐利。有平底。

071

龙 行 红 山
The Dragon Flies along
the Mountains

龙腾中国：红山文化古国文明
Legends of Dragon：
The Ancient Civilization of Hongshan Culture

33. 泥塑仿木建筑构件

红山文化（距今约 6500-5000 年）

1983-1985 年辽宁省朝阳市凌源市牛河梁遗址第一地点"女神庙"出土（N1J1B:21）

残长 22.4 厘米，宽 19.0 厘米

辽宁省文物考古研究院藏

Clay Sculpture of a Wood-like Architectural Component

Hongshan Culture (ca. 6,500–5,000 BP)

Unearthed from the Goddess Temple, Locus No. 1, Niuheliang Site, Lingyuan, Chaoyang, Liaoning between 1983 and 1985 (N1J1B:21)

Length (remaining) of 22.4 cm, width 19.0 cm

Liaoning Provincial Institute of Cultural Relics and Archaeology

泥质。面上遗有多处涂朱痕。两侧棱边都显外接痕，其中一边外接痕呈台阶状。背面可见成束且较粗的禾草秸秆印痕两组。

34. 泥塑仿木建筑构件

红山文化（距今约 6500-5000 年）

1983-1985 年辽宁省朝阳市凌源市牛河梁遗址第一地点"女神庙"出土
N1J1A:50　宽 18.4 厘米，厚 5.8 厘米，压窝直径 1.2 厘米，窝深 0.5 厘米，秸秆宽 1.1 厘米
N1J1A:49　残长 34.0 厘米，宽 27.0 厘米，厚 6.2 厘米
辽宁省文物考古研究院藏

Clay Sculptures of Wood-like Architectural Components

Hongshan Culture (ca. 6,500–5,000 BP)

Unearthed from the Goddess Temple, Locus No. 1, Niuheliang Site, Lingyuan, Chaoyang, Liaoning between 1983 and 1985
N1J1A:50: Width 18.4 cm, thickness 5.8 cm, diameter of indent 1.2 cm, depth of indent 0.5 cm, width of straw 1.1 cm
N1J1A:49: Length (remaining) 34.0 cm, width 27.0 cm, thickness 6.2 cm
Liaoning Provincial Institute of Cultural Relics and Archaeology

073

龙 行 红 山
The Dragon Flies along
the Mountains

龙腾中国：红山文化古国文明
Legends of Dragon：
The Ancient Civilization of Hongshan Culture

　　泥质。一件保存有一侧棱边，压窝圆而较深，斜行排列成行，背面有斜行成排秸秆印痕，与正面成行压窝斜行方向一致。另一件断面可见为四层泥，各层泥面上均钻满成排的小圆窝。背面禾草秸秆印痕成束状。

35. 泥塑乳丁构件

红山文化（距今约 6500-5000 年）

1983-1985 年辽宁省朝阳市凌源市牛河梁遗址第一地点"女神庙"出土（N1J1B:13）
残长 39.0 厘米，宽 33.0 厘米，厚 5.0-13.0 厘米，乳丁直径 1.5-2.0 厘米
辽宁省文物考古研究院藏

Clay Sculpture of a Component with Nipple-shaped Decoration

Hongshan Culture (ca. 6,500–5,000 BP)

Unearthed from the Goddess Temple, Locus No. 1, Niuheliang Site, Lingyuan, Chaoyang, Liaoning between 1983 and 1985 (N1J1B:13)
Length (remaining) 39.0 cm, width 33.0 cm, thickness 5.0–13.0 cm, diameter of nipples 1.5–2.0 cm
Liaoning Provincial Institute of Cultural Relics and Archaeology

泥质。表面漫圆形，面上布满贴塑的乳丁，乳丁排成多行，由上到下渐小。

龙 行 红 山
The Dragon Flies along
the Mountains

『何以中国』文物考古大展系列
"The Essence of China," an Exhibition Series
of Cultural Relics and Archaeological Achievements

36. 泥质彩绘壁画残块

红山文化（距今约 6500-5000 年）

1983-1985 年辽宁省朝阳市凌源市牛河梁遗址第一地点"女神庙"出土

残长 6.5 厘米，宽 6.5 厘米

辽宁省文物考古研究院藏

Fragment of Painted Clay Murals

Hongshan Culture (ca. 6,500–5,000 BP)

Unearthed from the Goddess Temple, Locus No. 1, Niuheliang Site, Lingyuan, Chaoyang, Liaoning between 1983 and 1985

Height (remaining) 6.5 cm, width 6.5 cm

Liaoning Provincial Institute of Cultural Relics and Archaeology

075

龙 行 红 山
The Dragon Flies along
the Mountains

龙腾中国：红山文化古国文明
Legends of Dragon：
The Ancient Civilization of Hongshan Culture

泥质。一侧有整齐的边缘。表面绘深浅相间的赭色斜带状图案，带较宽。背面竖行秸秆较粗。

辽西地区史前人像崇拜传统具有深厚的根脉。红山文化人像数量较前代更多，制作也更为精细。不同祭祀遗址中人像规模存在差异，"女神庙"人像最为复杂、层次最多，是红山社会的"共祖"，其他地点所发现的人像则是更小社会单元各自崇拜的"个祖"，反映出红山文化祖先崇拜已进入较为发达的阶段。

红山文化神庙和人像类遗存见于东山嘴、牛河梁等遗址，人像以陶塑、泥塑、玉雕、石雕等手法制作，在祭坛、神庙等礼仪场所进行祭祀。人像塑造十分注重写实，是祖先崇拜信仰的反映，体现红山社会"人神一体"的世界观。红山社会以祖先崇拜为主的祭祀活动被后世传承，成为中华传统文化的重要内容。

076

龙 行 红 山
The Dragon Flies along
the Mountains

『何以中国』文物考古大展系列
"The Essence of China," an Exhibition Series
of Cultural Relics and Archaeological Achievements

"女神庙"遗址

37. 石雕人像

兴隆洼文化（距今约 8000-7000 年）

1988-1991 年内蒙古自治区赤峰市林西县白音长汗遗址 19 号房址出土
高 36.6 厘米，胸宽 10.8 厘米，最厚 15.7 厘米
内蒙古自治区文物考古研究院藏

Stone-carved Human Figure

Xinglongwa Culture (ca. 8,000–7,000 BP)

Unearthed from House Remains No. 19, Baiyinchanghan Site, Linxi, Chifeng, Inner Mongolia between 1988 and 1991

Height 36.6 cm, width of chest 10.8 cm, greatest thickness 15.7 cm

Inner Mongolia Institute of Cultural Relics and Archaeology

　　黑灰色硬质基岩制成。采用打、琢、磨制等加工技术。颅顶尖削，前额突出，双眼深陷，鼻翼较宽，颧骨丰隆，吻部略突，双臂下垂，作弓身蹲踞状。下端打制加工成楔形。微微隆起的腹部具备孕妇特征，表现出原始氏族社会对裸体女像的崇拜。

077

龙行红山
The Dragon Flies along
the Mountains

龙腾中国：红山文化古国文明
Legends of Dragon：
The Ancient Civilization of Hongshan Culture

38. 石雕人面

兴隆洼文化（距今约 8000-7000 年）

1988-1991 年内蒙古自治区赤峰市林西县白音长汗遗址出土
高 5.8 厘米，宽 4.4 厘米，厚 0.2-0.6 厘米
内蒙古自治区文物考古研究院藏

Stone-carved Human Face

Xinglongwa Culture (ca. 8,000–7,000 BP)

Unearthed from the Baiyinchanghan Site, Linxi, Chifeng, Inner Mongolia between 1988 and 1991
Height 5.8 cm, width 4.4 cm, thickness 0.2–0.6 cm
Inner Mongolia Institute of Cultural Relics and Archaeology

078

龙行红山
The Dragon Flies along
the Mountains

『何以中国』文物考古大展系列
"The Essence of China," an Exhibition Series
of Cultural Relics and Archaeological Achievements

　　红褐色石料磨制，呈椭圆形片状。正面上部磨刻出月牙形双眼，嘴部镶嵌蚌壳制作的牙齿。背面位于眼的上部磨一道横向凹槽，在其两端向侧边钻孔，在两侧边相对位置向背面斜向钻孔，两两贯通，用于穿挂之用。

079

龙 行 红 山
The Dragon Flies along
the Mountains

龙腾中国：红山文化古国文明
Legends of Dragon：
The Ancient Civilization of Hongshan Culture

南湾子北遗址石人像出土现场

39. 石人像

兴隆洼文化（距今约 8000-7000 年）

2016 年内蒙古自治区赤峰市翁牛特旗南湾子北遗址 4 号房址出土（2016NWNF4 ② :1）
高 46.4 厘米，最宽处 16.0 厘米，蚌片直径 1.3 厘米
赤峰学院博物馆藏

Stone Human Figure

Xinglongwa Culture (ca. 8,000–7,000 BP)

Unearthed from House Remains No. 4, North of the Nanwanzi Site, Ongniud Banner, Chifeng, Inner Mongolia in 2016 (2016NWNF4 ② :1)
Height 46.4 cm, greatest width 16.0 cm, diameter of clamshell 1.3 cm
Chifeng University Museum

石人头顶较平，略有外弧。面部刻画清晰，双眉弯曲，分界明显，双目圆睁，右眼内放有圆形带孔蚌片表示眼球。双耳外凸呈弧形。鼻为三角形，鼻头较宽，鼻梁隆起。嘴巴为圆形浅坑，内嵌半圆形蚌片，其上刻有浅槽表示牙齿。双手刻画明显，右手搭于上腹部，左手置于胸前。胸部有明显凸起的两圆点，应是乳房的表现。腹部未见隆起，下身表现不明显。人像背部内凹，正面略外凸，整体呈站立状。

40. 石人像

兴隆洼文化（距今约 8000-7000 年）

2016 年内蒙古自治区赤峰市翁牛特旗南湾子北遗址 4 号房址出土（2016NWNF4 ② :2）

高 32.0 厘米，最宽 16.2 厘米

赤峰学院博物馆藏

Stone Human Figure

Xinglongwa Culture (ca. 8,000–7,000 BP)

Unearthed from House Remains No. 4, North of the Nanwanzi Site, Ongniud Banner, Chifeng, Inner Mongolia in 2016 (2016NWNF4 ② :2)

Height 32.0 cm, greatest width 16.2 cm

Chifeng University Museum

石人头顶圆弧，面部五官清晰可辨。半圆形双眉相连，眉弓凸出。眼睛圆睁，三角形鼻外凸不明显，双手置于胸前，未见明显性别特征的表示，腹部及下肢未表现。正、背两面较为平整，底部呈尖楔状。

南湾子北遗址出土的两件石人像选材讲究，圆雕精琢，造型生动形象，应是雕琢前明确设计、精心选料的结果。石人像原应立置于灶后的居住面之上，面对灶址和门道。这是首次在兴隆洼文化房址内发现能够区分出男女的成对石雕人像，可能代表当时聚落内共同供奉的祖先形象，具有极高的考古价值和艺术价值，对于了解兴隆洼文化晚期的祖先崇拜等原始信仰具有重要意义。

41. 石雕神人像

兴隆洼文化（距今约 8000-7000 年）

2015 年辽宁省阜新市阜蒙县沙拉乡塔尺营子遗址出土
高 7.8 厘米，宽 4.4 厘米，厚 2.7 厘米
辽宁省文物考古研究院藏

Stone-carved Deity

Xinglongwa Culture (ca. 8,000–7,000 BP)

Unearthed from the Tachiyingzi Site, Shala Township, Fumeng, Fuxin, Liaoning in 2015
Height 7.8 cm, width 4.4 cm, thickness 2.7 cm
Liaoning Provincial Institute of Cultural Relics and Archaeology

灰色燧石质，长方体，磨制光滑。正面上部中心有阴刻人面图案，人面圆眼，长弯眉，山形鼻，窄平口，口的两侧有上下交错的獠牙，牙外侧以双弧线表现，并有向外的放射状长尖齿突。双目两侧各有三个近蛇形的"S"纹，其下为八行排列整齐的倒三角纹。下部刻有一道横线。

龙 行 红 山
The Dragon Flies along
the Mountains

「何以中国」文物考古大展系列
"The Essence of China," an Exhibition Series
of Cultural Relics and Archaeological Achievements

42. 石雕女神像

赵宝沟文化（距今约 7200-6500 年）

1983 年河北省承德市滦平县后台子遗址出土
高 32.7 厘米，肩宽 23.5 厘米
滦平县博物馆藏

Stone-carved Goddess

Zhaobaogou Culture (ca. 7,200–6,500 BP)

Unearthed from the Houtaizi Site, Luanping, Chengde, Hebei in 1983
Height 32.7 cm, width of shoulder 23.5 cm
Luanping County Museum

用辉长岩雕琢而成，体表略加磨制，雕法简单。裸体孕妇形像，体型笨拙，蹲坐姿，耳外凸，头无发，两眉粗隆，呈弧状，眼睛以一阴线表示，微睁，鼻略凸，呈三角形，闭口，嘴部略隆，曲肘，两手相对抚腹，胸部两侧有二乳头，腰腹宽肥，小腹及后腰隆鼓，臀部与尖形小石座相连，腿向内曲，脚相对。石雕女神像是原始氏族社会、母系氏族时期社会发展的重要标志，不仅具有历史考古价值，还具有较高的雕刻艺术史研究价值。是祖先或生育女神以及火神母的象征，被誉为"滦河流域的老祖母"。

083

龙 行 红 山
The Dragon Flies along
the Mountains

龙腾中国：红山文化古国文明
Legends of Dragon：
The Ancient Civilization of Hongshan Culture

43. 石雕女神像

赵宝沟文化（距今约 7200-6500 年）

1983 年河北省承德市滦平县后台子遗址出土
高 34.0 厘米，肩宽 17.0 厘米
滦平县博物馆藏

Stone-carved Goddess

Zhaobaogou Culture (ca. 7,200–6,500 BP)

Unearthed from the Houtaizi Site, Luanping, Chengde, Hebei in 1983

Height 34.0 cm, width of shoulder 17.0 cm

Luanping County Museum

龙 行 红 山
The Dragon Flies along
the Mountains

『何以中国』文物考古大展系列
"The Essence of China," an Exhibition Series
of Cultural Relics and Archaeological Achievements

　　辉绿岩雕琢而成，裸体孕妇形象，端坐式。面部右侧有铲伤，发型不明显。两眉粗隆，呈弧状。眼睛以阴刻线表示，微睁。鼻略凸，呈三角形。耳外凸，嘴部略隆，闭口。曲肘，手抚腹，胸部有两乳头，腰腹宽肥，小腹隆鼓，臀部与柱形小石座相连。腿向内曲，两脚相对。

085

龙 行 红 山
The Dragon Flies along
the Mountains

龙腾中国：红山文化古国文明
Legends of Dragon：
The Ancient Civilization of Hongshan Culture

"女神像"出土现场

44. 女神像

红山文化（距今约 6500-5000 年）

1983 年辽宁省朝阳市凌源市牛河梁遗址第一地点"女神庙"出土（N1J1B∶1）

残高 22.5 厘米，颜宽 16.5 厘米，通耳宽 23.5 厘米，眼眶长 6.2 厘米，两眼间距 3.0 厘米，鼻长 4.5 厘米，鼻宽 4.0 厘米，耳长 7.5 厘米，耳宽 3.5 厘米，嘴长 8.5 厘米，唇高起 2.0-2.5 厘米

辽宁省文物考古研究院藏

Goddess of Hongshan

Hongshan Culture (ca. 6,500–5,000 BP)

Unearthed from the Goddess Temple, Locus No. 1, Niuheliang Site, Lingyuan, Chaoyang, Liaoning in 1983 (N1J1B:1)

Height (remaining) 22.5 cm, width of face 16.5 cm, overall width (from ear to ear) 23.5 cm, length of eye orbit 6.2 cm, interorbital distance 3.0 cm, length of nose 4.5 cm, width of nose 4.0 cm, length of ear 7.5 cm, width of ear 3.5 cm, length of mouth 8.5 cm, protrusion of lip 2.0–2.5 cm

Liaoning Provincial Institute of Cultural Relics and Archaeology

头顶以上残缺，额顶有箍饰，鬓角部位有竖行的系带；眼嵌玉石为睛，玉石为滑石质，淡灰色，睛面圆鼓磨光，睛的背面作出钉状，深嵌入眼窝中，直径 2.3 厘米。鼻部残损。上唇以下为贴面，露出有表现牙齿的似蚌壳质贴物痕迹；右耳完整，耳轮简化，左耳残缺，近耳垂部位可见一穿孔，可能与穿系耳饰有关。头像的背面和下部均为残面，从背面的残面看，应是贴于庙的墙壁处，尚可见塑造时包以草束的支架痕迹，为一高浮雕的人像头部。

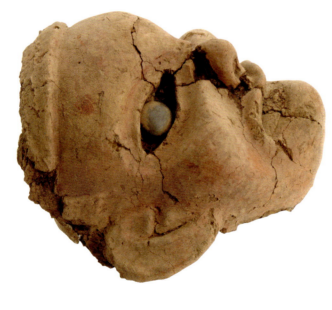

45. 泥塑耳部残件

红山文化（距今约 6500-5000 年）

1983-1985 年辽宁省朝阳市凌源市牛河梁遗址第一地点"女神庙"出土（N1J1B:16，N1J1B:30）
N1J1B:16 长 12.0 厘米，宽 6.4 厘米，厚 4.6 厘米
辽宁省文物考古研究院藏

Clay Sculptures (incomplete) of Ears

Hongshan Culture (ca. 6,500–5,000 BP)

Unearthed from the Goddess Temple, Locus No. 1, Niuheliang Site, Lingyuan, Chaoyang,
Liaoning between 1983 and 1985 (N1J1B:16, N1J1B:30)
N1J1B:16: Length 12.0 cm, width 6.4 cm, thickness 4.6 cm
Liaoning Provincial Institute of Cultural Relics and Archaeology

草拌泥质。表面较粗，一件正背面均可见捏塑痕，似为未塑完的半成品；另一件耳廓与耳轮的表现接近写实，耳垂较长。

088

龙 行 红 山
The Dragon Flies along
the Mountains

『何以中国』文物考古大展系列
"The Essence of China," an Exhibition Series
of Cultural Relics and Archaeological Achievements

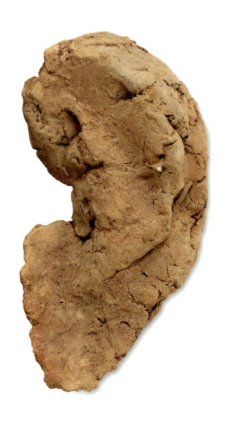

46. 泥塑手部残件

红山文化（距今约 6500-5000 年）

1983-1985 年辽宁省朝阳市凌源市牛河梁遗址第一地点"女神庙"出土（N1J1B:2）

通长 12.0 厘米，宽 9.5 厘米，高 4.0 厘米

辽宁省文物考古研究院藏

Clay Sculpture (incomplete) of a Hand

Hongshan Culture (ca. 6,500–5,000 BP)

Unearthed from the Goddess Temple, Locus No. 1, Niuheliang Site, Lingyuan, Chaoyang, Liaoning between 1983 and 1985 (N1J1B:2)

Overall length 12.0 cm, width 9.5 cm, height 4.0 cm

Liaoning Provincial Institute of Cultural Relics and Archaeology

草拌泥质。为左手，作握拳状。表面打磨光滑，四指收屈，拇指外伸，拇指尖稍显上翘。上端腕部扁圆中空。底部残断面较平，似托在一平面上。

089

龙 行 红 山
The Dragon Flies along
the Mountains

龙腾中国：红山文化古国文明
Legends of Dragon：
The Ancient Civilization of Hongshan Culture

47. 泥塑手部残件

红山文化（距今约 6500-5000 年）

1983-1985 年辽宁省朝阳市凌源市牛河梁遗址第一地点"女神庙"出土（N1J1B:4）

残长 22.0 厘米，宽 10.0 厘米

辽宁省文物考古研究院藏

Clay Sculpture (incomplete) of a Hand

Hongshan Culture (ca. 6,500–5,000 BP)

Unearthed from the Goddess Temple, Locus No. 1, Niuheliang Site, Lingyuan, Chaoyang, Liaoning between 1983 and 1985 (N1J1B:4)

Length (remaining) 22.0 cm, width 10.0 cm

Liaoning Provincial Institute of Cultural Relics and Archaeology

草拌泥质。为左手，作伸掌状。表面未精细打磨，五指伸张，不并拢，指细长，有指尖表现，拇指尖稍上翘，全手作按压状，手下部残断面较平。

090

龙 行 红 山
The Dragon Flies along
the Mountains

『何以中国』文物考古大展系列
"The Essence of China," an Exhibition Series
of Cultural Relics and Archaeological Achievements

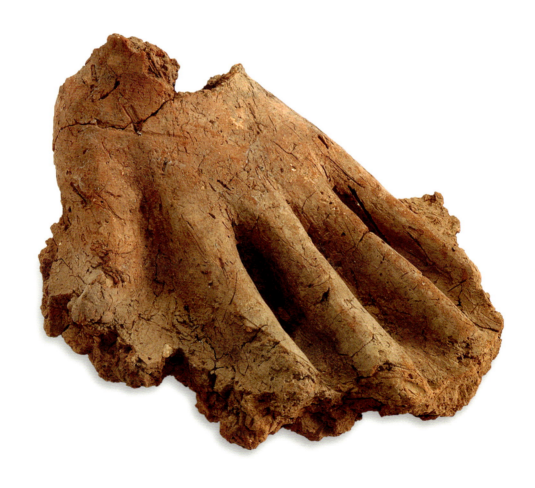

48. 泥塑乳房残件

红山文化（距今约 6500-5000 年）

1983-1985 年辽宁省朝阳市凌源市牛河梁遗址第一地点"女神庙"出土（N1J1B:6-1，N1J1B:6-2）

宽 13.0-13.5 厘米

辽宁省文物考古研究院藏

Clay Sculptures (incomplete) of Breasts

Hongshan Culture (ca. 6,500–5,000 BP)

Unearthed from the Goddess Temple, Locus No. 1, Niuheliang Site, Lingyuan, Chaoyang,

Liaoning between 1983 and 1985 (N1J1B:6-1, N1J1B:6-2)

Width 13.0–13.5 cm

Liaoning Provincial Institute of Cultural Relics and Archaeology

草拌泥质。表面打磨光滑，个体均较小，形状较丰满，无乳头表现。

091

龙 行 红 山
The Dragon Flies along
the Mountains

龙腾中国：红山文化古国文明
Legends of Dragon：
The Ancient Civilization of Hongshan Culture

49. 泥塑手臂残件

红山文化（距今约 6500-5000 年）

1983-1985 年辽宁省朝阳市凌源市牛河梁遗址第一地点"女神庙"出土（N1J1B:3）
残宽 25.5 厘米，上臂斜长 25.0 厘米，臂直径 9.0 厘米
辽宁省文物考古研究院藏

Clay Sculpture (incomplete) of an Arm

Hongshan Culture (ca. 6,500–5,000 BP)

Unearthed from the Goddess Temple, Locus No. 1, Niuheliang Site, Lingyuan, Chaoyang, Liaoning between 1983 and 1985 (N1J1B:3)

Width of fragment 25.5 cm, length of upper arm 25.0 cm, diameter of arm 9.0 cm

Liaoning Provincial Institute of Cultural Relics and Archaeology

草拌泥质。为左上臂连接左肩头及左前胸。表面压磨光滑，臂直而圆，有空腔，腔内遗有灰白色骨骼碎片，从下端残断处可见有向内收的趋势。左胸部正面平直，与臂相接处上部显圆肩，下部内里形成腋窝。

龙 行 红 山
The Dragon Flies along
the Mountains

『何以中国』文物考古大展系列
"The Essence of China," an Exhibition Series
of Cultural Relics and Archaeological Achievements

50. 陶塑人头像

红山文化（距今约 6500-5000 年）

2014-2016 年辽宁省朝阳市半拉山墓地出土（K18:1）

残高 3.5 厘米，头长 3.1 厘米，面阔 2.8 厘米

辽宁省文物考古研究院藏

Pottery Sculpture of a Human Head

Hongshan Culture (ca. 6,500–5,000 BP)

Unearthed from the Banlashan Cemetery, Chaoyang, Liaoning between 2014 and 2016 (K18:1)

Height (remaining) 3.5 cm, length of head 3.1 cm, width of face 2.8 cm

Liaoning Provincial Institute of Cultural Relics and Archaeology

093

龙 行 红 山

The Dragon Flies along
the Mountains

龙腾中国：红山文化古国文明

Legends of Dragon:
The Ancient Civilization of Hongshan Culture

泥质红褐陶，表面有一层斑驳的土沁皮。颈部以下残，断茬处满布土沁，应为早期残断。雕塑精致，表情生动。双眼微闭，呈一条月牙形窄缝。鼻子宽且短，鼻梁高挑。小口微张，两颊饱满。左耳残，右耳张开，耳廓较长。发髻采用刻划的短、细凹槽表现，顶部为三道环形相套的发髻，后枕部为三道与顶部相同的短弧形发髻，两侧和后部均为披肩发。颈部有一道竖向宽大的凹槽。

51. 石雕人头像

红山文化（距今约 6500-5000 年）

2014-2016 年辽宁省朝阳市半拉山墓地出土（T0503 ① :1）
高 14.2 厘米，头长 14.0 厘米，头宽 9.9 厘米
辽宁省文物考古研究院藏

Stone-carved Human Head

Hongshan Culture (ca. 6,500–5,000 BP)

Unearthed from the Banlashan Cemetery, Chaoyang, Liaoning between 2014 and 2016 (T0503 ① :1)
Height 14.2 cm, length 14.0 cm, width 9.9 cm
Liaoning Provincial Institute of Cultural Relics and Archaeology

　　黄褐色砂岩质，表面有一层土沁。保存基本完整，面部轮廓清晰。宽额头，高颧骨，矮鼻梁，圆鼻头，深眼窝，双目圆瞪、眼珠外凸，双唇紧闭，嘴角深陷，圆下颌前凸。左耳椭圆形，耳垂圆，右耳残。头顶中偏后部雕有椭圆盘形饰，推测为发髻或冠帽，后枕部平直。

52. 石雕人头像

红山文化（距今约 6500-5000 年）

2014-2016 年辽宁省朝阳市半拉山墓地 41 号墓出土（M41:1）

高 36.0 厘米，长 32.4 厘米，宽 9.6-13.8 厘米

辽宁省文物考古研究院藏

Stone-carved Human Head

Hongshan Culture (ca. 6,500–5,000 BP)

Unearthed from Tomb No. 41, Banlashan Cemetery, Chaoyang,
Liaoning between 2014 and 2016 (M41:1)

Height 36.0 cm, length 32.4 cm, width 9.6–13.8 cm

Liaoning Provincial Institute of Cultural Relics and Archaeology

　　黄褐色砂岩质，表面风化，有一层黑褐色土沁层。扁体，后脑部稍残，面部轮廓清晰。高额，顶部微凸，应为冠，头顶有拢冠带饰垂向脑后。耳部雕成半圆形，双目圆睁，外眼角斜向上，颧骨突出。鼻凸起呈三角形，鼻梁高耸，浅雕两鼻孔，嘴部微隆，闭口，嘴角及下颌雕刻数道胡须。

095

龙 行 红 山
The Dragon Flies along
the Mountains

龙腾中国：红山文化古国文明
Legends of Dragon：
The Ancient Civilization of Hongshan Culture

53. 石雕人像残件

红山文化（距今约 6500-5000 年）

2014-2016 年辽宁省朝阳市半拉山墓地 65 号墓出土（M65：1）
残高 16.9 厘米，残宽 15.6 厘米，厚 8.5 厘米
辽宁省文物考古研究院藏

Stone-carved Human Figure (incomplete)

Hongshan Culture (ca. 6,500–5,000 BP)

Unearthed from Tomb No. 65, Banlashan Cemetery, Chaoyang, Liaoning between 2014 and 2016 (M65:1)
Height (remaining) 16.9 cm, width (remaining) 15.6 cm, thickness 8.5 cm
Liaoning Provincial Institute of Cultural Relics and Archaeology

096

龙行红山
The Dragon Flies along
the Mountains

『何以中国』文物考古大展系列
"The Essence of China," an Exhibition Series
of Cultural Relics and Archaeological Achievements

　　黄褐色，含砾石粗砂岩质，表面有黑色土沁。底面雕刻较平整，应为半身像。现残存右侧小部分躯干，头、颈部和左侧残缺，背部保存较好。背挺直，肩后扳，右上臂紧贴身体，屈肘，手拇指张开、四指并拢，轻抚腹部，胸部圆鼓，腹部隆起前挺，从身姿形态推测此为孕妇像。右手手腕处以一组双勾直阴线表现装饰品。背部略呈弧形内凹，从背部可见残缺的左臂，双臂与身体相接处均以一道凹槽表示。

54. 陶塑人像残件

红山文化（距今约 6500-5000 年）

2014-2016 年辽宁省朝阳市半拉山墓地 29 号墓出土（M29：1）
残高 40.0 厘米，脐孔内径 4.0 厘米
辽宁省文物考古研究院藏

Pottery Sculpture (incomplete) of a Human Figure

Hongshan Culture (ca. 6,500–5,000 BP)

Unearthed from Tomb No. 29, Banlashan Cemetery, Chaoyang, Liaoning between 2014 and 2016 (M29:1)
Height (remaining) 40.0 cm, inner diameter of navel 4.0 cm
Liaoning Provincial Institute of Cultural Relics and Archaeology

泥质红陶，外表有一层陶衣，胎体厚重，应为裸体孕妇形象。头部和下肢残缺，仅存部分躯干和上肢。制作精良，通体打磨。人像大小与真人接近。双臂环抱于胸前，右手搭在左手臂上，左手不存，右手大拇指按在左臂内侧，其余四指并拢置于左臂外侧。鼓腹，腹中部脐眼外张，脐孔下斜。

097

龙 行 红 山
The Dragon Flies along
the Mountains

龙腾中国：红山文化古国文明
Legends of Dragon：
The Ancient Civilization of Hongshan Culture

55. 陶塑孕妇小像

红山文化（距今约 6500-5000 年）

1982 年辽宁省朝阳市喀左县东山嘴遗址出土（TD9 ② :7）

残高 5.1 厘米，宽 3.3 厘米

辽宁省文物考古研究院藏

Pottery Figurine of a Pregnant Woman

Hongshan Culture (ca. 6,500–5,000 BP)

Unearthed from the Dongshanzui Site, Kazuo, Chaoyang, Liaoning in 1982 (TD9 ② :7)

Height (remaining) 5.1 cm, width 3.3 cm

Liaoning Provincial Institute of Cultural Relics and Archaeology

泥质红陶，孕妇裸体立像，通体打磨光滑，似涂有红衣。头部及右臂残缺，腹部凸起，臀部肥大，左臂弯曲，左手贴于上腹，可见五指，有表现阴部的记号，下肢稍弯曲，足残。

56. 陶塑手部残件

红山文化（距今约 6500-5000 年）

1979 年辽宁省朝阳市喀左县东山嘴遗址出土
残长 14.5 厘米，宽 8.0 厘米
喀喇沁左翼蒙古族自治县博物馆藏

Pottery Sculpture (incomplete) of a Hand

Hongshan Culture (ca. 6,500–5,000 BP)

Unearthed from the Dongshanzui Site, Kazuo, Chaoyang, Liaoning in 1979
Length (remaining) 14.5 cm, width 8.0 cm
Harqin Left Wing Mongolian Autonomous County Museum

099

龙　行　红　山
The Dragon Flies along
the Mountains

龙腾中国：红山文化古国文明
Legends of Dragon :
The Ancient Civilization of Hongshan Culture

　　泥质红陶。该遗址出土了数件陶制人像，经复原，这类人像大约为真人的二分之一大小。该件文物为红山文化时期人体塑像的残件，仅存手臂部，右手握在左手之上。除了东山嘴遗址以外，在内蒙古自治区敖汉旗兴隆沟遗址发现的陶制人像保存相当完整，使我们可以一窥全貌。这类人像被认为是祖先的象征，用于祭祀。

57. 陶塑女性立像

红山文化（距今约 6500-5000 年）

1988 年辽宁省朝阳市凌源市牛河梁遗址第五地点二号冢出土（N5SCZ2∶4）

残高 9.6 厘米

辽宁省文物考古研究院藏

Pottery Sculpture of a Standing Woman

Hongshan Culture (ca. 6,500–5,000 BP)

Unearthed from Stone Mound No. 2, Locus No. 5, Niuheliang Site, Lingyuan, Chaoyang, Liaoning in 1988 (N5SCZ2:4)

Height (remaining) 9.6 cm

Liaoning Provincial Institute of Cultural Relics and Archaeology

100

龙 行 红 山
The Dragon Flies along
the Mountains

『何以中国』文物考古大展系列
"The Essence of China," an Exhibition Series
of Cultural Relics and Archaeological Achievements

　　立像，头部和右腿缺失。双乳凸起，双臂收拢贴于腹前，腹部微隆，背部向内凹进，背两侧有弧形线条，具有明显女性特征。人像通体压磨光滑，主体部分未见着有服饰，唯左足部塑出一半高靴形，靴与左脚形象都极为写实。

58. 石雕人像

红山文化（距今约 6500-5000 年）

2019 年辽宁省朝阳市建平县马鞍桥山遗址出土（T1843 ② :1）

高 2.4 厘米，宽 2.0 厘米

辽宁省文物考古研究院藏

Stone-carved Human Figure

Hongshan Culture (ca. 6,500–5,000 BP)

Unearthed from the Mount Ma'anqiao Site, Jianping, Chaoyang, Liaoning in 2019 (T1843 ② :1)

Height 2.4 cm, width 2.0 cm

Liaoning Provincial Institute of Cultural Relics and Archaeology

101

龙 行 红 山

龙腾中国：红山文化古国文明

The Dragon Flies along
the Mountains

Legends of Dragon：
The Ancient Civilization of Hongshan Culture

　　圆雕、镂空雕。通体磨制光滑。个体较小，细部雕刻较少，整体形象为一人双膝跪立像（踞坐像）。人像整体神态表现为双手紧扣、紧闭双目、静思遥想状。头部雕刻较简单，仅在面部浅雕出眼和嘴，现存右眼，嘴为一浅小的圆形凹坑。颈部为一道横向弯曲的沟槽，隔开头和躯干。颈后部与躯干之间由一个横向开放对钻的粗孔分隔开。右手臂镂空位于躯干前侧，手抚下腹部。双腿间由一道深沟槽分开，臀部与足部之间未完全分开。

59. 石雕人面

红山文化（距今约 6500-5000 年）

内蒙古自治区赤峰市敖汉旗七家村出土
长 2.6 厘米，宽 1.9 厘米，厚 0.8 厘米
赤峰博物院藏

Stone-carved Human Face

Hongshan Culture (ca. 6,500–5,000 BP)

Unearthed from Qijia Village, Aohan Banner, Chifeng, Inner Mongolia

Length 2.6 cm, width 1.9 cm, thickness 0.8 cm

Chifeng Museum

椭圆形，刻画出脸部轮廓及五官，脸部形象立体，一眼有残缺。

龙行红山
The Dragon Flies along
the Mountains

『何以中国』文物考古大展系列
"The Essence of China," an Exhibition Series
of Cultural Relics and Archaeological Achievements

60. 石雕人面残件

红山文化（距今约 6500-5000 年）

2001 年内蒙古自治区赤峰市敖汉旗草帽山遗址出土
残高 8.4 厘米，残宽 6.4 厘米，厚 2.7 厘米
敖汉博物馆（敖汉旗文物保护中心）藏

Stone-carved Human Face (incomplete)

Hongshan Culture (ca. 6,500–5,000 BP)

Unearthed from the Caomaoshan Site, Aohan Banner, Chifeng, Inner Mongolia in 2001
Height (remaining) 8.4 cm, width (remaining) 6.4 cm, thickness 2.7 cm
Aohan Museum (Aohan Banner Conservation Center of Cultural Relics)

103

龙 行 红 山
The Dragon Flies along
the Mountains

龙腾中国：红山文化古国文明
Legends of Dragon：
The Ancient Civilization of Hongshan Culture

　　红色凝灰岩质，雕琢而成。仅存额头下面、颈右半部，比真人略小，方脸，目微闭，鼻梁略高，嘴角微上扬，耳不甚明显。

61. 石雕人像

红山文化（距今约 6500-5000 年）

2001 年内蒙古自治区赤峰市敖汉旗草帽山遗址出土

残高 27.0 厘米，冠高 4.8 厘米，面高 18.0 厘米，面宽 14.0 厘米

敖汉博物馆（敖汉旗文物保护中心）藏

Stone-carved Human Figure

Hongshan Culture (ca. 6,500–5,000 BP)

Unearthed from the Caomaoshan Site, Aohan Banner, Chifeng, Inner Mongolia in 2001

Height (remaining) 27.0 cm, height of headdress 4.8 cm, height of face 18.0 cm, width of face 14.0 cm

Aohan Museum (Aohan Banner Conservation Center of Cultural Relics)

104

龙 行 红 山
The Dragon Flies along
the Mountains

「何 以 中 国」 文 物 考 古 大 展 系 列
"The Essence of China," an Exhibition Series
of Cultural Relics and Archaeological Achievements

　　红色凝灰岩质，雕琢而成。仅存完整头部和小部分胸部，比真人略小，方脸，头戴"凸"字形冠，双目微闭，高鼻梁，嘴唇略突出，嘴角微上扬，头部后刻出方形凸棱纹，垂肩，呈慈祥之态。

62. 石雕女神坐像

红山文化（距今约 6500-5000 年）

内蒙古自治区赤峰市境内出土
高 38.0 厘米，宽 22.0 厘米，厚 20.0 厘米
赤峰博物院藏

Stone-carved Statue of a Seated Goddess

Hongshan Culture (ca. 6,500–5,000 BP)

Unearthed from Chifeng, Inner Mongolia
Height 38.0 cm, width 22.0 cm, thickness 20.0 cm
Chifeng Museum

105

龙 行 红 山
The Dragon Flies along
the Mountains

龙腾中国：红山文化古国文明
Legends of Dragon：
The Ancient Civilization of Hongshan Culture

灰色凝灰岩质，圆雕，光头圆脸。阴刻线琢磨出双眼和凹槽形嘴，雕有双耳，脖下有一道圆环。裸体，露双乳，双手捧腹，孕妇状，倚坐在有靠背的圆形台尖上。

63. 巫觋像

红山文化（距今约 6500-5000 年）

1982 年内蒙古自治区赤峰市巴林右旗那日斯台遗址出土

高 19.1 厘米，宽 6.2 厘米，厚 5.0 厘米

巴林右旗博物馆藏

Statue of a Wizard

Hongshan Culture (ca. 6,500–5,000 BP)

Unearthed from the Narisitai Site, Bairin Right Banner, Chifeng, Inner Mongolia in 1982

Height 19.1 cm, width 6.2 cm, thickness 5.0 cm

Bairin Right Banner Museum

龙 行 红 山
The Dragon Flies along
the Mountains

『何以中国』文物考古大展系列
"The Essence of China," an Exhibition Series
of Cultural Relics and Archaeological Achievements

灰石质地。通体磨光。头顶有三重圆饼状装饰，顶部平齐。头部近菱形，面部造型十分抽象，三角形巨鼻，眉和眼极度下斜呈"八"字形，嘴部无明显饰痕。上身挺直，两手合于胸腹之前。束腰，跪坐，臀部压在双脚之上。

64. 玉坐人像

红山文化（距今约 6500-5000 年）

高 14.6 厘米，宽 6.0 厘米，厚 4.7 厘米

故宫博物院藏

Jade Statue of a Seated Human Figure

Hongshan Culture (ca. 6,500–5,000 BP)

Height 14.6 cm, width 6.0 cm, thickness 4.7 cm

The Palace Museum

黄绿色玉料制成，有大面积铁褐色沁斑。器形为一带动物冠的坐姿人像。人像裸身，尖下颚，蛋形首，面部窄而前凸，头上带一动物头形冠，动物眼睛圆凸，有两个竖直的长角，双耳镂空。动物两角之间有浅刻网格纹。人细腰长腿，以阴刻线刻画眼睛，呈坐姿，上肢弯曲抚于腿上。器背颈部有大的对穿孔，可以悬挂佩带。这件玉器展示着人戴着动物冠的形象，动物有角和眼睛，从形象看似鹿。经研究，此玉和牛河梁遗址第十六地点 4 号墓出土的裸身站立玉人以及英国剑桥大学菲茨威廉博物馆（Fitzwilliam Museum）收藏的披戴熊首熊身的倚坐玉人都是表现特定场合下的红山时代大巫的形象，是巫在行法时不同场景下的状态。玉人的主人很可能是一位身份地位极高且能通神独占的大巫，具有与天地、神灵沟通的能力，是远古人类天人合一的重要体现。

65. 红陶女神像

红山文化（距今约 6500-5000 年）

2001 年内蒙古自治区赤峰市松山区征集
高 14.6 厘米，宽 9.1 厘米，厚 7.0 厘米
内蒙古博物院藏

Red Pottery Statue of a Goddess

Hongshan Culture (ca. 6,500–5,000 BP)

Acquired from Songshan District, Chifeng, Inner Mongolia in 2001

Height 14.6 cm, width 9.1 cm, thickness 7.0 cm

Inner Mongolia Museum

龙 行 红 山
The Dragon Flies along
the Mountains

「何以中国」文物考古大展系列
"The Essence of China," an Exhibition Series
of Cultural Relics and Archaeological Achievements

　　陶质，褐色。写实手法塑造的女神陶塑像，仅残存头部。头部中空，头戴尖顶帽，帽上刻画出花纹，面部用镂空的短线刻画眼和嘴，眉毛处磨损，鼻梁细长突出，耳部呈弧状凹窝。写实手法浓郁，慈眉善目，尽现女性温柔之态。

　　红山文化最引人注目的文化特征之一，就是在大、小凌河流域的红山文化晚期遗址内发现了大大小小众多的陶塑人像和陶塑动物像。其中，陶塑人像多为女子形象，有的呈孕妇形象，有的头像有头饰、盘发等女体特征，凸显了红山文化发达的"女神崇拜"现象。

66. 人形陶壶

小河沿文化（距今约 5000-4000 年）

2008 年内蒙古自治区通辽市扎鲁特旗南宝力皋吐遗址出土

高 23.5 厘米，口径 15.6 厘米，腹径 39.2 厘米，底径 12.4 厘米

内蒙古自治区文物考古研究院藏

Human-shaped Pottery Pot

Xiaoheyan Culture (ca. 5,000–4,000 BP)

Unearthed from the Nanbaoligaotu Site, Jarud Banner, Tongliao, Inner Mongolia in 2008

Height 23.5 cm, diameter of rim 15.6 cm, diameter of belly 39.2cm, diameter of base 12.4 cm

Inner Mongolia Institute of Cultural Relics and Archaeology

　　红褐色细砂质陶，表面涂泥磨光，局部因烧制不匀留有黑斑块。敞口高领，圆鼓腹，平底，下腹部装饰对称的桥形耳。壶领内折，呈倒三角斜面，在面上堆塑，刻划五官，显现出清秀的面容。胸部堆塑对称的双乳，腹部鼓凸，臀部外耸，是典型的女性孕育形象，应是一尊有所寓意的偶像。

龙 行 红 山
The Dragon Flies along
the Mountains

『何以中国』文物考古大展系列
"The Essence of China," an Exhibition Series
of Cultural Relics and Archaeological Achievements

牛河梁遗址第二地点和祭坛航拍图

111

龙 行 红 山
The Dragon Flies along
the Mountains

龙腾中国：红山文化古国文明
Legends of Dragon：
The Ancient Civilization of Hongshan Culture

敬天 Worship of Heaven

112

龙 行 红 山

The Dragon Flies along
the Mountains

『何以中国』文物考古大展系列

"The Essence of China," an Exhibition Series
of Cultural Relics and Archaeological Achievements

天地崇拜观念与红山文化旱作农业文明走向成熟密切相关。红山文化先民为祈求风调雨顺和农业丰收，筑坛祭祀天地，通过观测天象，掌握自然规律，获得天文知识，形成系统的天地崇拜观念，遵循相同的祭祀礼仪规范。红山文化先民将"天圆地方"的理念融入祭坛的规划设计之中，夯筑土丘作为祭坛基础，外围包砌石墙和彩陶筒形器，各遗址祭坛样式和规模的差异体现出礼仪活动的层级化。

The concept of worshipping the heavens and the earth is closely related to the maturation of the Hongshan Culture's dryland agriculture. To pray for favorable weather and bountiful harvests, the Hongshan people built altars to offer sacrifices to the heavens and the earth. By observing celestial phenomena, they grasped natural laws, acquired astronomical knowledge, developed a conceptual system of worshipping the heavens and the earth, and followed a set of sacrificial and ritual norms. The people incorporated the idea of "the heavens are round and the earth is square" into the location and design of their altars, with rammed earth mounds as the base and with stone walls and painted pottery cylinders enclosing the area. The differences in altar styles and sizes across the various sites reflect the hierarchical nature of ritual activities.

彩陶筒形器是红山文化特有的器物，均为泥制红陶，中空无底，上下贯通，通常半面施有彩绘。这类器物见于祭坛与积石冢，成排立置，是特殊的祭祀礼器，具有贯通天地的功能。

牛河梁遗址第二地点四号冢筒形器出土现场

113

龙 行 红 山
The Dragon Flies along
the Mountains

龙腾中国：红山文化古国文明
Legends of Dragon：
The Ancient Civilization of Hongshan Culture

67. 陶筒形器

红山文化（距今约 6500-5000 年）

1985-1988 年辽宁省朝阳市凌源市牛河梁遗址第一地点第三建筑址出土（N1J3:8）
高 60.6 厘米，口径 23.2 厘米
辽宁省文物考古研究院藏

Pottery Cylinder

Hongshan Culture (ca. 6,500–5,000 BP)

Unearthed from Architecture Remains No. 3, Locus No. 1, Niuheliang Site, Lingyuan, Chaoyang, Liaoning between 1985 and 1988 (N1J3:8)
Height 60.6 cm, diameter of rim 23.2 cm
Liaoning Provincial Institute of Cultural Relics and Archaeology

泥质红陶。厚圆唇，短折领，领下凹弦纹较疏朗，腹壁较直，底内沿起台。为牛河梁遗址第一地点第三建筑址出土可复原筒形器中腹部最长的一件。

龙 行 红 山
The Dragon Flies along
the Mountains

『何以中国』文物考古大展系列
"The Essence of China," an Exhibition Series
of Cultural Relics and Archaeological Achievements

68. 彩陶筒形器

红山文化（距今约 6500-5000 年）

辽宁省朝阳市建平县牛河梁遗址第二地点四号冢出土（N2Z4A：20）

高 59.7 厘米，口径 32.0 厘米，腹径 36.5 厘米，底径 34.2 厘米

辽宁省文物考古研究院藏

Painted Pottery Cylinder

Hongshan Culture (ca. 6,500–5,000 BP)

Unearthed from Stone Mound No. 4, Locus No. 2, Niuheliang Site, Jianping, Chaoyang, Liaoning (N2Z4A:20)

Height 59.7 cm, diameter of rim 32.0 cm, diameter of belly 36.5 cm, diameter of base 34.2 cm

Liaoning Provincial Institute of Cultural Relics and Archaeology

泥质红陶，饰黑彩。直口，筒腹，最大腹径偏下。圆唇，卷沿。口下饰 12 厘米宽凹弦纹带。腹部菱形方格纹带下接垂鳞纹。

69. 彩陶筒形器

红山文化（距今约 6500-5000 年）

辽宁省朝阳市建平县牛河梁遗址第二地点四号冢出土（N2Z4L：1）

高 47.0 厘米，口径 26.0 厘米，腹径 31.0 厘米，底径 25.0 厘米

辽宁省文物考古研究院藏

Painted Pottery Cylinder

Hongshan Culture (ca. 6,500–5,000 BP)

Unearthed from Stone Mound No. 4, Locus No. 2, Niuheliang Site, Jianping, Chaoyang, Liaoning (N2Z4L:1)

Height 47.0 cm, diameter of rim 26.0 cm, diameter of belly 31.0 cm, diameter of base 25.0 cm

Liaoning Provincial Institute of Cultural Relics and Archaeology

泥质红陶，饰黑彩。通体器壁匀称向外弧鼓，最大腹径位于器中腹处。口沿近宽平，稍内斜，底部微内收，底内沿面有弧曲。从口沿下至下腹部饰勾连涡纹四组。

116

龙 行 红 山
The Dragon Flies along
the Mountains

『何以中国』文物考古大展系列
"The Essence of China," an Exhibition Series
of Cultural Relics and Archaeological Achievements

70. 彩陶筒形器

红山文化（距今约 6500-5000 年）

辽宁省朝阳市建平县牛河梁遗址第二地点四号冢出土（N2Z4B:3）

高 22.0 厘米，口径 23.5 厘米，底径 23.0 厘米

辽宁省文物考古研究院藏

Painted Pottery Cylinder

Hongshan Culture (ca. 6,500–5,000 BP)

Unearthed from Stone Mound No. 4, Locus No. 2, Niuheliang Site, Jianping, Chaoyang, Liaoning (N2Z4B:3)

Height 22.0 cm, diameter of rim 23.5 cm, diameter of base 23.0 cm

Liaoning Provincial Institute of Cultural Relics and Archaeology

龙 行 红 山

The Dragon Flies along
the Mountains

『何以中国』文物考古大展系列

"The Essence of China," an Exhibition Series
of Cultural Relics and Archaeological Achievements

　　泥质红陶，饰黑彩。口径与腹径相近。圆唇，口沿圆凸，底内沿削平。口沿下绘两条连续菱形方格纹饰带。

71. 彩陶筒形器

红山文化（距今约 6500-5000 年）

1985-1988 年辽宁省朝阳市凌源市牛河梁遗址第一地点第三建筑址出土（N1J3：10）

口径 32.5 厘米，底径 33.2 厘米

辽宁省文物考古研究院藏

Painted Pottery Cylinder

Hongshan Culture (ca. 6,500–5,000 BP)

Unearthed from Architecture Remains No. 3, Locus No. 1, Niuheliang Site, Lingyuan, Chaoyang, Liaoning between 1985 and 1988 (N1J3:10)

Diameter of rim 32.5 cm, diameter of base 33.2 cm

Liaoning Provincial Institute of Cultural Relics and Archaeology

120

龙 行 红 山

The Dragon Flies along
the Mountains

『何以中国』文物考古大展系列

"The Essence of China," an Exhibition Series
of Cultural Relics and Archaeological Achievements

　　泥质红陶，饰黑彩。下部残。圆唇，口外敞，领较短。凹弦纹较细而整齐，凸棱下以黑彩绘直角三角纹。

72. 扁钵式陶筒形器

红山文化（距今约 6500-5000 年）

辽宁省朝阳市建平县牛河梁遗址第二地点一号冢出土（N2Z1）

高 10.2 厘米，口径 23.7 厘米

辽宁省文物考古研究院藏

Pottery Cylinder in the Shape of Flat *Bo* (food vessel)

Hongshan Culture (ca. 6,500–5,000 BP)

Unearthed from Stone Mound No. 1, Locus No. 2, Niuheliang Site, Jianping, Chaoyang, Liaoning (N2Z1)

Height 10.2 cm, diameter of rim 23.7 cm

Liaoning Provincial Institute of Cultural Relics and Archaeology

泥质红陶。圆唇较薄，折肩处显凸棱，微鼓腹。绘黑彩，纹样不清。

121

龙 行 红 山
The Dragon Flies along
the Mountains

龙腾中国：红山文化古国文明
Legends of Dragon：
The Ancient Civilization of Hongshan Culture

尊王 Ritual Privileges

积石冢是红山文化特有的埋葬形式。大冢建于山冈之巅，层层叠起，如同后世"山陵"景观。积石冢群、单个冢和冢墓葬排列有序，等级分明，秩序俨然，反映红山社会金字塔式分层结构。每个积石冢中心大墓与周围中、小墓葬等级分化明显，凸显了中心大墓主人"独尊"的王者地位。

The stone mound tomb is a unique burial form of the Hongshan Culture. The big tomb was constructed on a hilltop, with layers of stones piled up, looking very much like the mountain mausoleum of later times. The tomb clusters, individual tombs, and the order of burials reflect the hierarchy of Hongshan society. The central, large burial pit in each stone-mounded tomb is distinctly differentiated from its surrounding medium-sized and small burial pits, highlighting the "sole supremacy" of the person interred in the central pit.

『何以中国』文物考古大展系列
"The Essence of China," an Exhibition Series
of Cultural Relics and Archaeological Achievements

73. 彩陶罍

红山文化（距今约 6500-5000 年）

1993 年辽宁省朝阳市建平县牛河梁遗址第二地点四号冢 6 号墓出土（N2Z4M6：1）

通高 49.2 厘米

罐体高 42.36 厘米，口径 13.2 厘米，腹径 42.4 厘米，底径 12.0 厘米

盖高 7.2 厘米，径 18.9 厘米

辽宁省文物考古研究院藏

Painted Pottery *Lei* (wine vessel)

Hongshan Culture (ca. 6,500–5,000 BP)

Unearthed from Tomb No. 6, Stone Mound No. 4, Locus No. 2, Niuheliang Site, Jianping, Chaoyang, Liaoning in 1993 (N2Z4M6:1)

Overall height 49.2 cm

Height of body 42.36 cm, diameter of rim 13.2 cm, diameter of belly 42.4 cm, diameter of base 12.0 cm

Height of lid 7.2 cm, diameter of lid 18.9 cm

Liaoning Provincial Institute of Cultural Relics and Archaeology

泥质红陶。敛口，圆唇，领甚短，圆肩，大圆鼓腹，小平底，下腹侧附竖桥状双耳。器表通体饰红陶衣，从肩到下腹部绘四道宽带黑彩勾连涡纹。器盖似倒置陶钵，圆顶，正顶部嵌一桥状小钮，绘四道黑彩，为平行线间斜宽带纹。

123

龙 行 红 山
The Dragon Flies along
the Mountains

龙腾中国：红山文化古国文明
Legends of Dragon：
The Ancient Civilization of Hongshan Culture

74. 彩陶罍及陶钵

红山文化（距今约 6500-5000 年）

1996 年辽宁省朝阳市建平县牛河梁遗址第二地点四号冢 7 号墓出土（N2Z4M7∶1，N2Z4M7∶2）

罍通高 29.5 厘米，口径 12.4 厘米，腹径 36.4 厘米，底径 10.5 厘米

钵高 6.4 厘米，口径 22.4 厘米，底径 6.8 厘米

辽宁省文物考古研究院藏

Painted Pottery *Lei* (wine vessel) and Pottery *Bo* (food vessel)

Hongshan Culture (ca. 6,500–5,000 BP)

Unearthed from Tomb No. 7, Stone Mound No. 4, Locus No. 2, Niuheliang Site,

Jianping, Chaoyang, Liaoning in 1996 (N2Z4M7:1, N2Z4M7:2)

Lei: overall height 29.5 cm, diameter of rim 12.4 cm, diameter of belly 36.4 cm, diameter of base 10.5 cm

Bo: height 6.4 cm, diameter of rim 22.4 cm, diameter of base 6.8 cm

Liaoning Provincial Institute of Cultural Relics and Archaeology

龙 行 红 山

The Dragon Flies along
the Mountains

『何以中国』文物考古大展系列

"The Essence of China:" an Exhibition Series
of Cultural Relics and Archaeological Achievements

　　罍为泥质红陶。敛口，沿甚短，方圆唇，广肩，圆鼓腹，平底，腹径大于器高，整体显扁圆。中腹附竖桥状双耳。器表涂红陶衣，肩至腹部绘多组似无勾的黑彩涡纹。

　　钵亦为泥质红陶。口微敛，方圆唇，底略内凹。此钵当作为罍的器盖使用。

75. 彩陶盖罐

红山文化（距今约 6500-5000 年）

1988 年辽宁省朝阳市凌源市牛河梁遗址第十地点出土（N10:1）

通高 27.0 厘米，口径 13.5 厘米，盖径 17.5 厘米

辽宁省文物考古研究院藏

Painted Pottery Jar with a Lid

Hongshan Culture (ca. 6,500–5,000 BP)

Unearthed from Locus No. 10, Niuheliang Site, Lingyuan, Chaoyang, Liaoning in 1988 (N10:1)

Overall height 27.0 cm, diameter of rim 13.5 cm, diameter of lid 17.5 cm

Liaoning Provincial Institute of Cultural Relics and Archaeology

泥质红陶。由罐和盖组成。罐直口、鼓腹、平底，上腹部有两个系耳。饰三组带状勾连花卉纹。盖弧顶，有一桥状钮。分内外两圈纹饰，内圈以内弧线和四组对称的梭形黑彩形成中心的方形阳纹图案，外圈由五组对弧线三角黑彩扩出五组梭形阳纹图案。

125

龙 行 红 山
The Dragon Flies along
the Mountains

龙腾中国：红山文化古国文明
Legends of Dragon :
The Ancient Civilization of Hongshan Culture

76. 陶双耳罐及陶盖盘

红山文化（距今约 6500-5000 年）

1996 年辽宁省朝阳市建平县牛河梁遗址第二地点四号冢 8 号墓出土（N2Z4M8：2，N2Z4M8：3）

罐高 40.8 厘米，口径 22.0 厘米，底径 10.0 厘米

盘高 8.5 厘米，口径 31.8 厘米，底径 8.0 厘米

辽宁省文物考古研究院藏

Double-handled Pottery Jar and Pottery Tray with a Lid

Hongshan Culture (ca. 6,500–5,000 BP)

Unearthed from Tomb No. 8, Stone Mound No. 4, Locus No. 2, Niuheliang Site,

Jianping, Chaoyang, Liaoning in 1996 (N2Z4M8:2, N2Z4M8:3)

Jar: height 40.8 cm, diameter of rim 22.0 cm, diameter of base 10.0 cm

Tray: height 8.5 cm, diameter of rim 31.8 cm, diameter of base 8.0 cm

Liaoning Provincial Institute of Cultural Relics and Archaeology

　　罐为泥质红陶。敞口，直领外折，折处内起锐棱，方唇。溜肩，鼓腹，器身瘦高，小平底。桥形双耳位于中腹偏下。

　　盘为泥质黑陶。敞口，方圆唇较薄，中腹曲折，折处内壁起锐棱、外壁圆棱，小底近平。近底部凿一孔，孔呈不规则椭圆形。

龙 行 红 山

The Dragon Flies along
the Mountains

『何以中国』文物考古大展系列

"The Essence of China," an Exhibition Series
of Cultural Relics and Archaeological Achievements

77. 彩陶盖罐

红山文化（距今约 6500-5000 年）

2011 年辽宁省朝阳市凌源市田家沟墓地 8 号墓出土（M8∶2）

通高 19.3 厘米，口径 16.5 厘米，底径 11.0 厘米

辽宁省文物考古研究院藏

Painted Pottery Jar with a Lid

Hongshan Culture (ca. 6,500–5,000 BP)

Unearthed from Tomb No. 8, Tianjiagou Cemetery, Lingyuan, Chaoyang, Liaoning in 2011 (M8:2)

Overall height 19.3 cm, diameter of rim 16.5 cm, diameter of base 11.0 cm

Liaoning Provincial Institute of Cultural Relics and Archaeology

泥质红陶。由罐和盖组成。罐直口、矮领、鼓腹、平底，上腹部有两个系耳。通体饰横向条纹与斜带状纹相间的纹饰。盖平顶，顶部有一个桥状捉手，饰"十"字形纹饰。

78. 彩陶三足盖罐

红山文化（距今约 6500-5000 年）

辽宁省朝阳市凌源市田家沟墓地 4 号墓出土（T3M4：3）

通高 16.24 厘米

盖高 2.88 厘米，口径 11.76 厘米

罐高 13.36 厘米，口径 12.20 厘米，最大腹径 21.46 厘米，底径 15.00 厘米，足高 2.62 厘米

辽宁省文物考古研究院藏

Painted Pottery Tripod Jar with a Lid

Hongshan Culture (ca. 6,500–5,000 BP)

Unearthed from Tomb No. 4, Tianjiagou Cemetery, Lingyuan, Chaoyang, Liaoning (T3M4:3)

Overall height of jar with lid 16.24 cm

Lid: height 2.88 cm, diameter of rim 11.76 cm

Jar: height 13.36 cm, diameter of rim 12.20 cm, greatest diameter of belly 21.46 cm, diameter of base 15.00 cm, height of foot 2.62 cm

Liaoning Provincial Institute of Cultural Relics and Archaeology

泥质红陶。由罐和盖组成。罐直口、矮领、鼓腹，有三个片状足，近似圈足。上腹部有两个系耳。通体饰横向条纹，纹饰脱落不清晰。盖弧顶，有桥状捉手。

129

龙 行 红 山
The Dragon Flies along
the Mountains

龙腾中国：红山文化古国文明
Legends of Dragon：
The Ancient Civilization of Hongshan Culture

牛河梁遗址第十六地点位于遗址群西南，东北距"女神庙"五千余米，分布1座积石冢。4号墓位于冢内中心，由封石、封土及积石层构成，石棺以17层花岗岩板精砌，随葬高规格玉器组合，是目前所发现的红山文化时期规模最大、规格最高的一座大型石棺墓，充分反映出该墓主人的"一人独尊"式的社会地位。

130

龙 行 红 山
The Dragon Flies along
the Mountains

『何以中国』文物考古大展系列
"The Essence of China:" an Exhibition Series
of Cultural Relics and Archaeological Achievements

79. 玉凤

红山文化（距今约 6500-5000 年）

2002 年辽宁省朝阳市凌源市牛河梁遗址第十六地点 4 号墓出土（N16M4:1）

长 20.43 厘米，宽 12.71 厘米，厚 1.24 厘米

辽宁省文物考古研究院藏

Jade Phoenix

Hongshan Culture (ca. 6,500–5,000 BP)

Unearthed from Tomb No. 4, Locus No. 16, Niuheliang Site, Lingyuan, Chaoyang, Liaoning in 2002 (N16M4:1)

Length 20.43 cm, width 12.71 cm, thickness 1.24 cm

Liaoning Provincial Institute of Cultural Relics and Archaeology

淡绿色玉质。整体呈扁薄板状，正面中间略鼓，周边较薄，背面较平。平面形状近长方形，具流线形外廓。正面作卧姿，回首，弯颈，高冠，圆睛，疣鼻，喙扁且长，前端钩曲，与羽翅相接。颈长且粗壮，不见羽毛的表现；圆睛中间高，周围低，目先雕作三棱体；前额疣突发达，鼻尖附近见一椭圆形凹面，应为鼻孔；喙沟作成减地沟槽状，槽底线十分规整；颈、头和身体之间使用镂透技法，正面浅磨，背面深磨，中间镂透，身侧开槽较陡，颈侧开槽略缓；飞羽和尾羽区域占了身体的绝大部分，羽翅略呈圆状。

131

龙 行 红 山
The Dragon Flies along
the Mountains

龙腾中国：红山文化古国文明
Legends of Dragon :
The Ancient Civilization of Hongshan Culture

80. 斜口筒形玉器

红山文化（距今约 6500-5000 年）

2002 年辽宁省朝阳市凌源市牛河梁遗址第十六地点 4 号墓出土（N16M4：2）

高 13.7 厘米，平口长径 6.9 厘米，短径 5.9 厘米，斜口最宽 8.45 厘米，壁厚 0.45-0.52 厘米

辽宁省文物考古研究院藏

Cylindrical Jade Vessel with an Oblique Rim

Hongshan Culture (ca. 6,500–5,000 BP)

Unearthed from Tomb No. 4, Locus No. 16, Niuheliang Site, Lingyuan, Chaoyang, Liaoning in 2002 (N16M4:2)

Height 13.7 cm, longer diameter of flat rim 6.9 cm, shorter diameter of flat rim 5.9 cm,

greatest width of oblique rim 8.45 cm, thickness of wall 0.45–0.52 cm

Liaoning Provincial Institute of Cultural Relics and Archaeology

龙行红山
The Dragon Flies along
the Mountains

『何以中国』文物考古大展系列
"The Essence of China:" an Exhibition Series
of Cultural Relics and Archaeological Achievements

　　淡绿色玉质，绿中泛黄，有铁锈红色瑕斑。器体呈扁圆筒状，通体抛光。一端为宽大的斜口，腹壁外敞；一端为稍窄的平口，两侧面近平口端各单面钻一小孔。两端开口缘部较薄，局部有残损的小缺口。斜口与平口内壁的正中部位隐约可见内凹的线切割痕迹。

81. 玉镯

红山文化（距今约 6500-5000 年）

2002 年辽宁省朝阳市凌源市牛河梁遗址第十六地点 4 号墓出土（N16M4:3）

直径 7.6 厘米，孔径 6.0 厘米，厚 0.9 厘米

辽宁省文物考古研究院藏

Jade Bracelet

Hongshan Culture (ca. 6,500–5,000 BP)

Unearthed from Tomb No. 4, Locus No. 16, Niuheliang Site, Lingyuan, Chaoyang, Liaoning in 2002 (N16M4:3)

Diameter 7.6 cm, diameter of hole 6.0 cm, thickness 0.9 cm

Liaoning Provincial Institute of Cultural Relics and Archaeology

淡绿色玉质，泛黄白色，有较多白色瑕斑。通体磨制精致，光素无纹。形制规整，平面近正圆形。内缘面不平，外缘起棱，横截面呈不规则的圆角三角形。

133

龙 行 红 山
The Dragon Flies along
the Mountains

龙腾中国：红山文化古国文明
Legends of Dragon:
The Ancient Civilization of Hongshan Culture

82. 玉人

红山文化（距今约 6500-5000 年）

2002 年辽宁省朝阳市凌源市牛河梁遗址第十六地点 4 号墓出土（N16M4：4）

高 18.5 厘米，头宽 4.42 厘米，脚宽 2.88 厘米，厚 2.34 厘米

辽宁省文物考古研究院藏

Jade Human Figure

Hongshan Culture (ca. 6,500–5,000 BP)

Unearthed from Tomb No. 4, Locus No. 16, Niuheliang Site, Lingyuan, Chaoyang, Liaoning in 2002 (N16M4:4)

Height 18.5 cm, width of head 4.42 cm, width of foot 2.88 cm, thickness 2.34 cm

Liaoning Provincial Institute of Cultural Relics and Archaeology

龙 行 红 山
The Dragon Flies along
the Mountains

『何 以 中 国』文 物 考 古 大 展 系 列
"The Essence of China," an Exhibition Series
of Cultural Relics and Archaeological Achievements

　　淡绿色玉质，细密坚硬。玉人为整身形象，立姿，通体抛光。形体为圆缓三面体，有正、背面之分。正面由左右两个平面在中部呈棱脊状接合而成，略显圆厚；背面由一个微弧面组成，稍显平缓。正面半圆雕，上宽下窄，外轮廓线较为平直，在颈部、腰部、踝部以减地沟槽、宽阴线等内束方式将人体分为头、胸腹、腿、足四部分，各部分转折圆缓，凹缺处均呈"V"形。头较大，圆脸，粗颈，斜肩，细腰，阔臀，双腿并立，圆尖状双足。背面光素无纹饰，仅在斜立双足中部见一阴刻线，将双足分开；背面还见有大面积深浅不一的铁锈红瑕斑，左侧尤其明显。左侧头顶局部有略呈圆形的玉皮痕。在颈部两侧和背面见有三孔，孔壁穿系磨损痕不明显。

83. 玉环

红山文化（距今约 6500-5000 年）

2002 年辽宁省朝阳市凌源市牛河梁遗址第十六地点 4 号墓出土
N16M4：5　直径 6.55 厘米，孔径 5.53 厘米，厚 0.5 厘米
N16M4：6　直径 6.6 厘米，孔径 5.5 厘米，厚 0.45 厘米
辽宁省文物考古研究院藏

Jade Rings

Hongshan Culture (ca. 6,500–5,000 BP)

Unearthed from Tomb No. 4, Locus No. 16, Niuheliang Site, Lingyuan, Chaoyang, Liaoning in 2002
N16M4:5: Diameter 6.55 cm, diameter of hole 5.53 cm, thickness 0.5 cm
N16M4:6: Diameter 6.6 cm, diameter of hole 5.5 cm, thickness 0.45 cm
Liaoning Provincial Institute of Cultural Relics and Archaeology

　　均为淡绿色玉质，绿中泛黄，应为同一玉料制作。通体光素无纹，微瑕。形制规整，平面近正圆形。内缘厚，外缘边薄起棱，横截面呈圆角三角形。其中一件内缘有残损。

龙 行 红 山

The Dragon Flies along
the Mountains

『何以中国』文物考古大展系列

"The Essence of China," an Exhibition Series
of Cultural Relics and Archaeological Achievements

84. 绿松石坠饰

红山文化（距今约 6500–5000 年）

2002 年辽宁省朝阳市凌源市牛河梁遗址第十六地点 4 号墓出土
N16M4：7　直径 1.9 厘米，高 0.74 厘米，厚 0.12 厘米
N16M4：8　直径 1.8 厘米，高 0.74 厘米，厚 0.13 厘米
辽宁省文物考古研究院藏

Turquoise Pendants

Hongshan Culture (ca. 6,500–5,000 BP)

Unearthed from Tomb No. 4, Locus No. 16, Niuheliang Site, Lingyuan, Chaoyang, Liaoning in 2002
N16M4:7: Diameter 1.9 cm, height 0.74 cm, thickness 0.12 cm
N16M4:8: Diameter 1.8 cm, height 0.74 cm, thickness 0.13 cm
Liaoning Provincial Institute of Cultural Relics and Archaeology

绿松石质，一件绿中泛蓝，另一件为纯绿色。两件坠饰小巧精制，通体磨光，形制相同，应为一对。背面均未附黑皮，片状，甚平整，近半圆形，底部直边两端外凸，弧形上缘正中单面桯钻一细圆孔。

137

龙 行 红 山
The Dragon Flies along
the Mountains

龙腾中国：红山文化古国文明
Legends of Dragon：
The Ancient Civilization of Hongshan Culture

牛河梁遗址第五地点位于遗址群中心地带，东北距"女神庙"约二千米，分布3座积石冢。一号冢中心大墓1号墓主体为大型土圹，四壁分设台阶，石棺以长条形石板平砌构建，棺壁每侧叠砌六至七层石板，顶部以大块石板叠搭为盖，盖板上方覆封石。

龙行红山
The Dragon Flies along
the Mountains

『何以中国』文物考古大展系列
"The Essence of China," an Exhibition Series
of Cultural Relics and Archaeological Achievements

85. 玉璧

红山文化（距今约 6500-5000 年）

1987 年辽宁省朝阳市凌源市牛河梁遗址第五号地点一号冢 1 号墓出土（N5Z1M1:2）

最大外径 12.0 厘米，内孔径 3.9 厘米

辽宁省文物考古研究院藏

Jade *Bi* (disc)

Hongshan Culture (ca. 6,500–5,000 BP)

Unearthed from Tomb No. 1, Stone Mound No. 1, Locus No. 5, Niuheliang Site, Lingyuan, Chaoyang, Liaoning in 1987 (N5Z1M1:2)

Greatest outer diameter 12.0 cm, diameter of inner hole 3.9 cm

Liaoning Provincial Institute of Cultural Relics and Archaeology

绿色，一侧布满白色斑痕。整体呈长圆形。内外缘磨薄似刃，内缘稍厚，体中部厚而圆鼓，
上边缘钻双孔。

139

龙 行 红 山
The Dragon Flies along
the Mountains

龙腾中国：红山文化古国文明
Legends of Dragon :
The Ancient Civilization of Hongshan Culture

86. 鼓形玉箍

红山文化（距今约 6500-5000 年）

1987 年辽宁省朝阳市凌源市牛河梁遗址第五号地点一号冢 1 号墓出土（N5Z1M1:3）

高 4.2 厘米，孔径 6.1 厘米

辽宁省文物考古研究院藏

Drum-shaped Jade Hoop

Hongshan Culture (ca. 6,500–5,000 BP)

Unearthed from Tomb No. 1, Stone Mound No. 1, Locus No. 5, Niuheliang Site, Lingyuan, Chaoyang, Liaoning in 1987 (N5Z1M1:3)

Height 4.2 cm, diameter of hole 6.1 cm

Liaoning Provincial Institute of Cultural Relics and Archaeology

龙 行 红 山
The Dragon Flies along
the Mountains

「何以中国」文物考古大展系列
"The Essence of China," an Exhibition Series
of Cultural Relics and Archaeological Achievements

黄绿色，圆润光泽。箍体较高，正圆口，内壁平直，外壁圆凸如鼓。虽造型简单，但形体甚为规整，磨制精工，是牛河梁遗址出土红山文化玉器中的一件珍品。

87. 勾云形玉器

红山文化（距今约 6500-5000 年）

1987 年辽宁省朝阳市凌源市牛河梁遗址第五号地点一号冢 1 号墓出土（N5Z1M1:4）

长 20.9 厘米，宽 12.4 厘米

辽宁省文物考古研究院藏

Hooked-cloud-shaped Jade Object

Hongshan Culture (ca. 6,500–5,000 BP)

Unearthed from Tomb No. 1, Stone Mound No. 1, Locus No. 5, Niuheliang Site, Lingyuan, Chaoyang, Liaoning in 1987 (N5Z1M1:4)

Length 20.9 cm, width 12.4 cm

Liaoning Provincial Institute of Cultural Relics and Archaeology

141

龙 行 红 山
The Dragon Flies along
the Mountains

龙腾中国：红山文化古国文明
Legends of Dragon：
The Ancient Civilization of Hongshan Culture

淡绿色，间有片状瑕斑。体呈长方形，四角作向外卷勾状，勾尖均不显，在中心盘卷的卷勾端部与器体相交处尚保存有制作镂孔时的圆孔状，正面磨出与卷勾走向相应的瓦沟纹，瓦沟纹较浅。背面无纹，有 4 个对钻的隧孔。

88. 玉镯

红山文化（距今约 6500-5000 年）

1987 年辽宁省朝阳市凌源市牛河梁遗址第五地点一号冢 1 号墓出土（N5Z1M1:5）

直径 8.5 厘米，孔径 6.5 厘米，厚 1.1 厘米

辽宁省文物考古研究院藏

Jade Bracelet

Hongshan Culture (ca. 6,500–5,000 BP)

Unearthed from Tomb No. 1, Stone Mound No. 1, Locus No. 5, Niuheliang Site, Lingyuan, Chaoyang, Liaoning in 1987 (N5Z1M1:5)

Diameter 8.5 cm, diameter of hole 6.5 cm, thickness 1.1 cm

Liaoning Provincial Institute of Cultural Relics and Archaeology

黄绿色玉质，有白色瑕斑。通体磨制精致。形制甚为规整，平面正圆形。镯体稍厚，内缘面平，外缘起圆棱，横截面为圆三角形。

龙 行 红 山
The Dragon Flies along
the Mountains

『何以中国』文物考古大展系列
"The Essence of China," an Exhibition Series
of Cultural Relics and Archaeological Achievements

89. 玉鳖

红山文化（距今约 6500-5000 年）

1987 年辽宁省朝阳市凌源市牛河梁遗址第五号地点一号冢 1 号墓出土
N5Z1M1：6　长 9.0 厘米，宽 7.7 厘米，厚 1.9 厘米
N5Z1M1：7　长 9.4 厘米，宽 8.5 厘米，厚 2.0 厘米
辽宁省文物考古研究院藏

Jade Soft-shelled Turtles

Hongshan Culture (ca. 6,500–5,000 BP)

Unearthed from Tomb No. 1, Stone Mound No. 1, Locus No. 5, Niuheliang Site, Lingyuan, Chaoyang, Liaoning in 1987
N5Z1M1:6: Length 9.0 cm, width 7.7 cm, thickness 1.9 cm
N5Z1M1:7: Length 9.4 cm, width 8.5 cm, thickness 2.0 cm
Liaoning Provincial Institute of Cultural Relics and Archaeology

分别出土于墓主人左、右手部位，黄绿色。首部形状近于三角形，有以起地阳纹和短阴线技法雕出的目和口，纹均甚浅，隐约可见，微缩颈，屈肢，有尾，四肢以较细的阴线雕出，背稍凸起，平腹。

胡头沟遗址1号墓作为次级聚落积石冢中心大墓，形制和随葬品与牛河梁遗址中心大墓等级差异明显，为探究红山文明内部社会复杂化进程提供了重要线索。

90. 玉璧

红山文化（距今约 6500-5000 年）

1973 年辽宁省阜新市胡头沟遗址 1 号墓出土（M1:1）

直径 4.0 厘米

辽宁省博物馆藏

Jade *Bi* (disc)

Hongshan Culture (ca. 6,500–5,000 BP)

Unearthed from Tomb No. 1, Hutougou Site, Fuxin, Liaoning in 1973 (M1:1)

Diameter 4.0 cm

Liaoning Provincial Museum

145

龙 行 红 山
The Dragon Flies along
the Mountains

龙腾中国：红山文化古国文明
Legends of Dragon:
The Ancient Civilization of Hongshan Culture

　　乳白色玉质，质地坚硬。平面近方圆形，中部稍厚，外边缘薄似刀刃。线条流畅，璧中央有一大圆孔，边缘有一小孔。作为"六器"之一，玉璧象征天，或代表对月亮的崇拜，与牛河梁祭坛遗址发现的祭天仪轨相符。该玉璧很可能是红山文化晚期祭祀体系中的重要礼器，兼具神权象征与身份标识功能。其独特形制与工艺展现了红山先民对玉材质感的敏锐把握及宗教仪轨的独特理解，是红山文化精神信仰与工艺技术的典型代表。

91. 玉环

红山文化（距今约 6500-5000 年）

1973 年辽宁省阜新市胡头沟遗址 1 号墓出土（M1:2）

外径 4.6 厘米，内径 3.5 厘米

辽宁省博物馆藏

Jade Ring

Hongshan Culture (ca. 6,500–5,000 BP)

Unearthed from Tomb No. 1, Hutougou Site, Fuxin, Liaoning in 1973 (M1:2)

Outer diameter 4.6 cm, inner diameter 3.5 cm

Liaoning Provincial Museum

　　玉呈白色，局部有黄土沁。环体纤细近圆形，有凸起的棱线，断面呈菱形。整体断为多段，已修复。玉环或者玉镯是红山文化随葬品中出现频率最高的一类器型，其他所有类型玉器几乎都可与之共出，是当时最基本的器类，很可能具有身份识别功能，即可视为墓主人身份的一种标志物。并且镯与环存在着彼此替代的过程，也就是说镯的出现早于环，这也为红山文化晚期的阶段性变化提供新的视角。

92. 玉龟

红山文化（距今约 6500-5000 年）

1973 年辽宁省阜新市胡头沟遗址 1 号墓出土（M1:6）

长 4.8 厘米，宽 2.8 厘米

辽宁省博物馆藏

Jade Tortoise

Hongshan Culture (ca. 6,500–5,000 BP)

Unearthed from Tomb No. 1, Hutougou Site, Fuxin, Liaoning in 1973 (M1:6)

Length 4.8 cm, width 2.8 cm

Liaoning Provincial Museum

龙 行 红 山
The Dragon Flies along
the Mountains

『何以中国』文物考古大展系列
"The Essence of China," an Exhibition Series
of Cultural Relics and Archaeological Achievements

　　淡绿色玉质，质地温润细腻，局部可见黄褐色土沁，符合红山文化玉器"就地取材"的特点。玉龟体细长，呈伸头爬行状，三角形头部微抬，尖尾内收，捕捉龟类运动瞬间的鲜活姿态，突破静态造型的程式化限制。头部以阴刻线勾勒口、目，线条简练传神；背部通体抛光，与腹面突脊的粗犷线条形成对比，展现"粗中有细"的技法平衡。腹面纵向突脊两侧对称穿孔，孔道内壁光滑，可穿系。

　　龟在古代巫术中被视为沟通天地的媒介，其腹甲常用于占卜，此器或为祭祀时"灵龟附体"的象征载体。龟的冬眠习性被赋予"生死循环"的隐喻，也与红山积石冢反映的祖先崇拜密切相关。凌家滩文化出土的玉龟夹玉版组合，与红山玉龟存在造型与功能的相似性，暗示新石器时代晚期燕辽与江淮地区的宗教观念存在一定交流。

93. 玉龟

红山文化（距今约 6500-5000 年）

1973 年辽宁省阜新市胡头沟遗址 1 号墓出土（M1:7）

长 3.9 厘米，最宽 3.6 厘米，厚 0.9 厘米

辽宁省文物考古研究院藏

Jade Tortoise

Hongshan Culture (ca. 6,500–5,000 BP)

Unearthed from Tomb No. 1, Hutougou Site, Fuxin, Liaoning in 1973 (M1:7)

Length 3.9 cm, greatest width 3.6 cm, thickness 0.9 cm

Liaoning Provincial Institute of Cultural Relics and Archaeology

淡绿色。首部形状近于三角形，颈前伸，龟背近椭圆，屈肢，有尾，无其他细部表现，腹面正中一竖脊，脊正中横穿一孔。

147

龙 行 红 山
The Dragon Flies along
the Mountains

龙腾中国：红山文化古国文明
Legends of Dragon：
The Ancient Civilization of Hongshan Culture

94. 玉鸮

红山文化（距今约 6500-5000 年）

1973 年辽宁省阜新市胡头沟遗址 1 号墓出土（M1:9）

高 3.1 厘米，宽 3.1 厘米

辽宁省博物馆藏

Jade Owl

Hongshan Culture (ca. 6,500–5,000 BP)

Unearthed from Tomb No. 1, Hutougou Site, Fuxin, Liaoning in 1973 (M1:9)

Height 3.1 cm, width 3.1 cm

Liaoning Provincial Museum

龙 行 红 山
The Dragon Flies along
the Mountains

『何以中国』文物考古大展系列
"The Essence of China:" an Exhibition Series
of Cultural Relics and Archaeological Achievements

　　淡绿色，质地温润细腻，部分区域可见白沁或自然沁色，表面呈现哑光或油质光泽。玉鸮呈展翅飞翔状，双翅向两侧展开，表现出动态张力。这种造型可能模仿了鸮类（猫头鹰）捕猎时的姿态，反映了红山先民对自然生物的细致观察。相较于其他红山玉鸟（如牛河梁遗址的玉凤），这件玉鸮翅膀比例较窄且线条简练，体现红山玉器"以形写神"的抽象化表现手法。可能与当时玉料切割工艺或图腾象征需求相关。尾部作扇形展开，与翅膀形成平衡构图，增强了视觉稳定感。鸮在红山文化中被视为沟通天地的媒介，玉鸮多出土于高等级墓葬，暗示其与原始宗教或萨满教仪式的关联。也可能与《山海经》中"鸱鸮司夜"的神话观念存在渊源。同墓地仅少数墓葬随葬玉鸮，表明持有者具有特殊社会地位，或为部落祭司阶层成员。该玉鸮的考古价值不仅在于其艺术成就，更揭示了红山文化玉礼器系统的早期形态，为研究中国北方地区史前社会复杂化进程提供了重要物证。

95. 玉鸮

红山文化（距今约 6500-5000 年）

1973 年辽宁省阜新市胡头沟遗址 1 号墓出土（M1:8）

高 2.4 厘米，宽 4.6 厘米

辽宁省博物馆藏

Jade Owl

Hongshan Culture (ca. 6,500–5,000 BP)

Unearthed from Tomb No. 1, Hutougou Site, Fuxin, Liaoning in 1973 (M1:8)

Height 2.4 cm, width 4.6 cm

Liaoning Provincial Museum

　　淡绿色，质地温润，表面有自然沁色和光泽，因少抛光而呈现哑光感。玉鸮正面双翅展开呈对称状，尾部宽大。背面横穿一孔以便于系挂。头部雕琢出圆眼和凸起的耳部（猫头鹰的耳羽簇）。翅膀和尾部用阴刻细线表现羽毛，虽线条简练，但符合红山文化"以线代面"的抽象风格。玉鸮是红山文化中晚期动物题材玉器的典型造型。红山文化崇尚自然神灵，鸮被视为通天神鸟。

96. 玉棒

红山文化（距今约 6500-5000 年）

1973 年辽宁省阜新市胡头沟遗址 1 号墓出土（M1∶10）

残长分别为 30.9 厘米、27.4 厘米、18.5 厘米、14.9 厘米、7.4 厘米、4.0 厘米、2.4 厘米

辽宁省文物考古研究院藏

Jade Rods

Hongshan Culture (ca. 6,500–5,000 BP)

Unearthed from Tomb No. 1, Hutougou Site, Fuxin, Liaoning in 1973 (M1:10)

Lengths (remaining): 30.9 cm, 27.4 cm, 18.5 cm, 14.9 cm, 7.4 cm, 4.0 cm, 2.4 cm

Liaoning Provincial Institute of Cultural Relics and Archaeology

白色。棒状，截面呈正圆形，通体磨光。

龙 行 红 山
The Dragon Flies along
the Mountains

『何以中国』文物考古大展系列
"The Essence of China:" an Exhibition Series
of Cultural Relics and Archaeological Achievements

半拉山遗址集墓葬与祭祀遗存于一体，12号墓是积石冢东南部次中心大墓，墓圹为圆角长方形竖穴土坑，石棺盖板、四壁和底板俱全。墓内随葬玦形玉龙、玉璧与石钺，体现军权与王权的结合。

龙 行 红 山

The Dragon Flies along
the Mountains

『何以中国』文物考古大展系列

"The Essence of China," an Exhibition Series
of Cultural Relics and Archaeological Achievements

97. 玦形玉龙

红山文化（距今约 6500-5000 年）

2014-2016 年辽宁省朝阳市半拉山墓地 12 号墓出土（M12:1）

高 13.5 厘米，宽 10.1 厘米，厚 3.3 厘米，孔径 3.2-4.3 厘米

辽宁省文物考古研究院藏

Jade Dragon in the Shape of *Jue* (slit ring)

Hongshan Culture (ca. 6,500–5,000 BP)

Unearthed from Tomb No. 12, Banlashan Cemetery, Chaoyang, Liaoning between 2014 and 2016 (M12:1)

Height 13.5 cm, width 10.1 cm, thickness 3.3 cm, diameter of hole 3.2–4.3 cm

Liaoning Provincial Institute of Cultural Relics and Archaeology

淡绿色微泛黄的透闪石玉，质地细腻，夹杂大量细小白色杂质。两侧面有白色瑕斑，背部有数道裂纹，并有多处未打磨平的疤痕，体扁平厚重，整体莹润有光泽。猪龙形，龙体卷曲如环，头尾相离似玦。龙体光滑无纹饰，首部雕刻精美。长立耳，耳廓宽大高耸。双目圆睁、微鼓，吻部前凸，两侧鼻孔微张，嘴紧闭。前额与鼻之间刻有五道宽大阴线，其眉间三道阴线与眼眶线相通，鼻部由两道阴线表现，嘴部为一道阴线。环孔由两侧对钻而成，对钻稍有偏差，孔缘经打磨，圆而光滑。背上部钻一细孔，孔径不规则。通体精磨，形制规整，制作精致。

98. 石钺

红山文化（距今约 6500-5000 年）

2014-2016 年辽宁省朝阳市半拉山墓地 12 号墓出土（M12:2）

长 13.7 厘米，宽 10.3 厘米，厚 1.3 厘米

辽宁省文物考古研究院藏

Stone *Yue* (axe)

Hongshan Culture (ca. 6,500–5,000 BP)

Unearthed from Tomb No. 12, Banlashan Cemetery, Chaoyang, Liaoning between 2014 and 2016 (M12:2)

Length 13.7 cm, width 10.3 cm, thickness 1.3 cm

Liaoning Provincial Institute of Cultural Relics and Archaeology

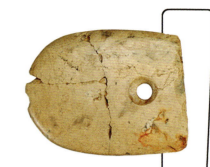

土黄色石质。磨制。残破为三块，可复原。质地细腻，一侧有红色土沁斑块。平面为舌状，近似截半的椭圆形，体扁平。顶端平直略斜，两侧边略外弧，与圆弧的刃部自然相接。顶部有两侧对打形成的疤痕面，未进行打磨，便于镶嵌入木柄内。两侧边刃部较厚，刃部稍薄，不锋利，均未见使用痕迹。钺体上部对钻一孔。

龙 行 红 山
The Dragon Flies along
the Mountains

『何以中国』文物考古大展系列
"The Essence of China," an Exhibition Series
of Cultural Relics and Archaeological Achievements

玉兽首端饰

红山文化（距今约 6500-5000 年）

2014-2016 年辽宁省朝阳市半拉山墓地 12 号墓出土（M12：4）
长 6.1 厘米，宽 4.5 厘米，厚 2.4 厘米
辽宁省文物考古研究院藏

Animal-head-shaped Jade Finial

Hongshan Culture (ca. 6,500–5,000 BP)

Unearthed from Tomb No. 12, Banlashan Cemetery, Chaoyang, Liaoning between 2014 and 2016 (M12:4)
Length 6.1 cm, width 4.5 cm, thickness 2.4 cm
Liaoning Provincial Institute of Cultural Relics and Archaeology

　　乳白色玉石质，微泛灰。磨制。表面光滑，较润泽。体呈楔形，一端厚重，雕刻出兽首形，一端渐薄，加工出榫头。兽首雕刻精美，双耳直立，耳廓圆润，双目是一对钻的穿孔，两侧钻孔稍偏差，孔不规则，额头微耸，圆短吻，鼻尖上翘，口微张，下颌宽厚，颈部内收出棱，下接楔形榫头，表面未打磨。

99. 玉璧

红山文化（距今约 6500-5000 年）

2014-2016 年辽宁省朝阳市半拉山墓地 12 号墓出土（M12:3）
长 14.5 厘米，宽 13.3 厘米，孔长 6.0 厘米，孔宽 5.5 厘米，厚 0.7 厘米
辽宁省文物考古研究院藏

Jade *Bi* (disc)

Hongshan Culture (ca. 6,500–5,000 BP)

Unearthed from Tomb No. 12, Banlashan Cemetery, Chaoyang, Liaoning between 2014 and 2016 (M12:3)
Length 14.5 cm, width 13.3 cm, length of hole 6.0 cm, width of hole 5.5 cm, thickness 0.7 cm
Liaoning Provincial Institute of Cultural Relics and Archaeology

龙 行 红 山

The Dragon Flies along
the Mountains

『何以中国』文物考古大展系列

"The Essence of China," an Exhibition Series
of Cultural Relics and Archaeological Achievements

　　绿色微泛黄的透闪石玉质，局部有白色云絮状沁，有绺裂。残破为三块，可复原。方形璧，体宽大、扁平。内、外轮廓边缘薄，横截面近梭形。一侧长边中部有两孔，以一面钻为主，并对两孔的两侧面进行了二次加工，一侧两孔之间打磨出横向连接的凹槽，另一侧两孔各自打磨出斜向上方的凹槽。通体精磨，形制规整，制作精致。

157

龙 行 红 山
The Dragon Flies along
the Mountains

龙腾中国：红山文化古国文明
Legends of Dragon :
The Ancient Civilization of Hongshan Culture

龙衍九州 The Dragon Hovers over China

　　西辽河流域史前文化有制玉、用玉的深厚根基。红山文化在形成的发展过程中，继承了兴隆洼文化和赵宝沟文化传统，将玉器雕琢技术推向新的高度。红山文化晚期，社会内部分化，等级制度确立，礼仪活动趋于复杂，进一步促成了中国最早玉礼制系统的形成。以玉龙为代表的动物形玉雕、勾云形器、斜口筒形器和方圆形玉璧为主的玉器组合，构成了红山古国文明的重要内涵和突出特征，影响远播黄河、长江流域。以玉为礼器和龙崇拜是红山文化重要的文明成就，也是中华五千年文明形成的重要标志之一，具有开创性意义。

　　The prehistoric cultures in the West Liao River basin boasted a profound heritage of jade crafting and usage. During its formation and development, the Hongshan Culture built upon the traditions of the Xinglongwa and Zhaobaogou cultures, advancing jade-carving techniques to new heights. In its late phase, Hongshan saw social stratification and the emergence of a hierarchical system, with ritual activities becoming more sophisticated. This further led to the establishment of China's earliest jade ritual system. Animal-shaped jade carvings represented by the jade dragon, hooked cloud-shaped jade artifacts, oblique-mouthed tubular jade artifacts, and combinations of square and round jade disks constituted a significant part of the civilization of Hongshan as an ancient state. Its cultural influence spread far and wide, reaching the basins of the Yellow and Yangtze rivers. The use of jade as ritual objects and the worship of dragons are not only remarkable achievements of the Hongshan Culture but also key markers of the very beginning of Chinese civilization, which occurred more than five thousand years ago.

玉礼　Order of Jade Rites

龙行九州

The Dragon Hovers
over China

『何以中国』文物考古大展系列

"The Essence of China," an Exhibition Series
of Cultural Relics and Archaeological Achievements

西辽河流域早期玉器出现于八千多年前，传承至红山文化晚期，数量明显增多，种类大为丰富。红山文化玉器器型源于实际生活的饰品、工具与武器，表现现实存在的生物以及幻想产生的抽象或变形物，制作和使用表现出一定的规范，玉器作为通神媒介、权力象征、礼制载体，寄托了红山社会共同的精神信仰。红山文化开创出中国史前玉器的鼎盛时代，形成了系统性的玉礼制度。

In the West Liao River basin, jade artifacts first appeared over 8,000 years ago and continued into the late Hongshan Culture, where they increased substantially in number and variety. Hongshan jade artifacts originated from ornaments, tools, and weapons in daily life, as well as from real animals and abstract or transformed creatures of imagination. Their production and usage followed certain standards. As a medium for communicating with the divine, a symbol of power, and a carrier of the ritual system, they embodied the shared spirit and beliefs of the whole community. The Hongshan Culture ushered in the golden age of China's prehistoric jade artifacts and established a ritual system based on jade.

以玉为美

　　红山文化继承和发展了东北地区以璧、环、玦、管、匕类器物为典型特征的玉文化传统，玉器种类增加、制玉工艺成熟和玉器制作使用规范化程度提高，成为红山文化玉礼器系统形成的重要基础。

100. 玉玦

兴隆洼文化（距今约 8000-7000 年）

1988-1991 年内蒙古自治区赤峰市林西县白音长汗遗址 4 号墓出土
直径 4.2-4.4 厘米，厚 1.0 厘米，孔径 0.9-1.5 厘米
内蒙古自治区文物考古研究院藏

Jade *Jue* (slit ring)

Xinglongwa Culture (ca. 8,000–7,000 BP)

Unearthed from Tomb No. 4, Baiyinchanghan Site, Linxi, Chifeng, Inner Mongolia between 1988 and 1991
Diameter 4.2–4.4 cm, thickness 1.0 cm, diameter of hole 0.9–1.5 cm
Inner Mongolia Institute of Cultural Relics and Archaeology

　　黄绿色玉，质地温润。器体较小略厚，平面为圆形，上下两面中部内凹，边缘最厚。中部单向钻有一个圆形孔。缺口呈长条形，内外宽窄相同。横剖面呈鼓形。

　　玉玦在新石器时代常作为耳饰使用，佩戴时将缺口处卡在耳朵上。同时，玉玦也可能具有一定的象征意义，代表着佩戴者的身份、地位或在部落中的角色等，是当时精神文化和审美观念的一种体现。

101. 玉管

兴隆洼文化（距今约 8000-7000 年）

1988-1991 年内蒙古自治区赤峰市林西县白音长汗遗址 4 号墓出土

长 3.8 厘米，直径 1.3-1.5 厘米，孔径 0.4-0.9 厘米

内蒙古自治区文物考古研究院藏

Jade Tube

Xinglongwa Culture (ca. 8,000–7,000 BP)

Unearthed from Tomb No. 4, Baiyinchanghan Site, Linxi, Chifeng, Inner Mongolia between 1988 and 1991

Length 3.8 cm, diameter 1.3–1.5 cm, diameter of hole 0.4–0.9 cm

Inner Mongolia Institute of Cultural Relics and Archaeology

　　黄绿色玉，质地较温润。一端平齐，一端斜口。横剖面呈不规则圆形。斜口长度不大，由斜口面中部单项钻一个圆孔，孔内布满螺纹凹槽。越向齐平端孔径越小，到齐平面孔不居中，偏向一侧。

102. 玉匕

兴隆洼文化（距今约 8000-7000 年）

1986-1994 年辽宁省阜新市查海遗址 54 号房遗址出土（94FCF54:1）

长 6.44 厘米，宽 1.22-1.4 厘米，厚 0.47 厘米

辽宁省文物考古研究院藏

Jade Dagger

Xinglongwa Culture (ca. 8,000–7,000 BP)

Unearthed from House Remains No.54, Chahai Site, Fuxin, Liaoning between 1986 and 1994 (94FCF54:1)

Length 6.44 cm, width 1.22–1.4 cm, thickness 0.47 cm

Liaoning Provincial Institute of Cultural Relics and Archaeology

　　乳白色玉石质，有淡绿斑。通体磨制光润，留有极浅的切割痕。长扁条体，上窄下宽，内凹外弧，弧面中部有崩痕，圆薄边。上端对钻孔残，断面经修磨，呈微平直、圆角，其下又有一孔，一侧钻透；下端作圆弧状，凹侧斜磨，略向外翻翘。

玉匕

兴隆洼文化（距今约 8000-7000 年）

1986-1994 年辽宁省阜新市查海遗址 54 号房遗址出土（94FCF54:2）

长 5.42 厘米，宽 1.24-1.3 厘米，厚 0.5 厘米

辽宁省文物考古研究院藏

Jade Dagger

Xinglongwa Culture (ca. 8,000–7,000 BP)

Unearthed from House Remains No.54, Chahai Site, Fuxin, Liaoning between 1986 and 1994 (94FCF54:2)

Length 5.42 cm, width 1.24–1.3 cm, thickness 0.5 cm

Liaoning Provincial Institute of Cultural Relics and Archaeology

　　乳白色玉石质，有深绿斑。通体磨制光润。长扁条体，内凹外弧，弧面较深，周缘薄。上端作平直圆角，一角边缘原缺，对钻一孔；下端作圆弧状，凹侧斜磨，略向外翻翘。

103. 玉牌饰

红山文化（距今约 6500-5000 年）

内蒙古自治区赤峰市翁牛特旗海金山遗址征集
长 4.4 厘米，宽 2.7-3.0 厘米，厚 0.1-0.5 厘米
翁牛特旗博物馆（翁牛特旗文物保护中心）藏

Jade Plaque Ornament

Hongshan Culture (ca. 6,500–5,000 BP)

Acquired from the Haijinshan Site, Ongniud Banner, Chifeng, Inner Mongolia

Length 4.4 cm, width 2.7–3.0 cm, thickness 0.1–0.5 cm

Ongniud Museum (Ongniud Banner Conservation Center of Cultural Relics)

龙 衍 九 州　The Dragon Hovers over China

『 何 以 中 国 』 文 物 考 古 大 展 系 列　"The Essence of China:" an Exhibition Series of Cultural Relics and Archaeological Achievements

　　黄色玉，质细腻莹润，底部有白色雾状水沁，透明度高。牌饰上端中间有单向钻孔，孔左右两面均有细砣琢出的阴刻线一条。器形呈长方形，上薄下厚。

104. 钩形玉佩饰

红山文化（距今约 6500-5000 年）

内蒙古自治区赤峰市翁牛特旗海金山遗址征集

高 2.6 厘米，宽 2.3 厘米，厚 0.3 厘米

翁牛特旗博物馆（翁牛特旗文物保护中心）藏

Hook-shaped Jade Ornament

Hongshan Culture (ca. 6,500–5,000 BP)

Acquired from the Haijinshan Site, Ongniud Banner, Chifeng, Inner Mongolia

Height 2.6 cm, width 2.3 cm, thickness 0.3 cm

Ongniud Museum (Ongniud Banner Conservation Center of Cultural Relics)

165

龙　衍　九　州
The Dragon Hovers
over China

龙腾中国：红山文化古国文明
Legends of Dragon :
The Ancient Civilization of Hongshan Culture

　　黄玉质，质地细腻莹润，光洁纯净，顶端右上角有白色雾状水沁，半透明。饰件上部有两个单向钻孔，通体光素无纹，有白絮状沁斑。

105. 钩形玉饰件

红山文化（距今约 6500-5000 年）

内蒙古自治区赤峰市翁牛特旗征集

高 6.5 厘米，最宽 1.0 厘米

翁牛特旗博物馆（翁牛特旗文物保护中心）藏

Hook-shaped Jade Ornament

Hongshan Culture (ca. 6,500–5,000 BP)

Acquired from Ongniud Banner, Chifeng, Inner Mongolia

Height 6.5 cm, greatest width 1.0 cm

Ongniud Museum (Ongniud Banner Conservation Center of Cultural Relics)

166

龙衍九州
The Dragon Hovers
over China

『何以中国』文物考古大展系列
"The Essence of China," an Exhibition Series
of Cultural Relics and Archaeological Achievements

青色玉，质细腻，杂有白色絮状纹理，半透明。头尾残断，器体薄片弯曲，曲度成弧，通体磨光，宽端有一穿孔，整器布满絮状沁。

106. 天河石坠饰

红山文化（距今约 6500-5000 年）

2014 年辽宁省朝阳市半拉山墓地出土（M7∶1，M14∶1，M29∶4，M29∶5，M30∶2）

长 1.3-2.8 厘米

辽宁省文物考古研究院藏

Amazonite Pendants

Hongshan Culture (ca. 6,500–5,000 BP)

Unearthed from the Banlashan Cemetery, Chaoyang, Liaoning in 2014 (M7:1, M14:1, M29:4, M29:5, M30:2)

Length 1.3–2.8 cm

Liaoning Provincial Institute of Cultural Relics and Archaeology

淡绿色。片状，圆形或水滴形，有的顶部有穿孔。

107. 匕形玉器

哈民文化（距今约 6000-5000 年）

2010-2012 年内蒙古自治区通辽市科尔沁左翼中旗哈民忙哈遗址 47 号房址出土

长 6.24 厘米，宽 2.25 厘米，厚 0.65 厘米

内蒙古自治区文物考古研究院

Dagger-shaped Jade Object

Hamin Culture (ca. 6,000–5,000 BP)

Unearthed from House Remains No. 47, Hamin Mangha Site, Horqin Left Wing Middle Banner,

Tongliao, Inner Mongolia between 2010 and 2012

Length 6.24 cm, width 2.25 cm, thickness 0.65 cm

Inner Mongolia Institute of Cultural Relics and Archaeology

绿色玉。外表光滑，微透明，呈弯弧的长条形。主体似瘦长的椭圆形，有束颈，上窄下宽，顶端有穿孔。

108. 瓦沟纹玉臂饰

红山文化（距今约 6500-5000 年）

1986 年辽宁省朝阳市凌源市牛河梁遗址第三地点 9 号墓出土（N3M9：2）

高 6.2 厘米，弧长 8.0 厘米，宽 3.0 厘米，厚 0.3 厘米

辽宁省文物考古研究院藏

Jade Arm Ornament with Tile-groove Pattern

Hongshan Culture (ca. 6,500–5,000 BP)

Unearthed from Tomb No. 9, Locus No. 3, Niuheliang Site, Lingyuan, Chaoyang, Liaoning in 1986 (N3M9:2)

Height 6.2 cm, length of arc 8.0 cm, width 3.0 cm, thickness 0.3 cm

Liaoning Provincial Institute of Cultural Relics and Archaeology

淡绿色。器身作弯板状，一端宽而另端窄，宽端有直边，窄端为弧边。器身外弧的外表磨出减地阳纹式的五道回字形瓦沟纹，瓦沟线条整齐而沟面匀称。

169

龙 衍 九 州
The Dragon Hovers
over China

龙腾中国：红山文化古国文明
Legends of Dragon：
The Ancient Civilization of Hongshan Culture

109. 钩形玉器

红山文化（距今约 6500-5000 年）

辽宁省文物总店征集
长 9.5 厘米，宽 3.1 厘米
辽宁省博物馆藏

Hook-shaped Jade Object

Hongshan Culture (ca. 6,500–5,000 BP)

Acquired from the Liaoning Cultural Relics Flagship Store
Length 9.5 cm, width 3.1 cm
Liaoning Provincial Museum

淡绿色，泛黄，有淡褐色瑕斑，较光泽，通体磨光。扁体，分钩形体、栏和柄三部分，钩形体较宽，边起棱线，栏起双棱，间隔较宽，直柄下端做出榫状，榫面穿一小孔。侧边、柄、栏有内外压地起棱的作法。

110. 异形玉璧

红山文化（距今约 6500-5000 年）

2014-2016 年辽宁省朝阳市半拉山墓地 39 号墓出土（M39:1）

直径 4.35 厘米，孔径 2.0 厘米，厚 0.26 厘米

辽宁省文物考古研究院藏

Irregular Jade *Bi* (disc)

Hongshan Culture (ca. 6,500–5,000 BP)

Unearthed from Tomb No. 39, Banlashan Cemetery, Chaoyang, Liaoning between 2014 and 2016 (M39:1)

Diameter 4.35 cm, diameter of hole 2.0 cm, thickness 0.26 cm

Liaoning Provincial Institute of Cultural Relics and Archaeology

青色玉石质，略带糖色，局部有白色瑕斑，体表有两道自然的裂纹，整体质地细腻润泽。璧体平面近圆形，扁平、轻薄，中部稍厚，边缘薄似刃，横截面近梭形。璧体外缘三等分处各凸出一个形制相似、大小不一的月牙形耳饰。通体磨制光滑。

111. 玉璧

红山文化（距今约 6500-5000 年）

2014 年辽宁省朝阳市半拉山墓地 36 号墓出土（M36:1）
长 5.3 厘米，宽 5.0 厘米，孔长径 2.8 厘米，孔短径 2.6 厘米，厚 0.4 厘米
辽宁省文物考古研究院藏

Jade *Bi* (disc)

Hongshan Culture (ca. 6,500–5,000 BP)

Unearthed from Tomb No. 36, Banlashan Cemetery, Chaoyang, Liaoning in 2014 (M36:1)
Length 5.3 cm, width 5.0 cm, longer diameter of hole 2.8 cm, shorter diameter of hole 2.6 cm, thickness 0.4 cm
Liaoning Provincial Institute of Cultural Relics and Archaeology

淡绿色。近圆角方形，内外缘磨薄，体中部略厚，上边缘钻一孔。

龙 衍 九 州
The Dragon Hovers
over China

『何 以 中 国』文 物 考 古 大 展 系 列
"The Essence of China," an Exhibition Series
of Cultural Relics and Archaeological Achievements

112. 玉璧

哈民文化（距今约 6000-5000 年）

2010-2012 年内蒙古自治区通辽市科尔沁左翼中旗哈民忙哈遗址 46 号房址出土

长 7.45 厘米，宽 6.32 厘米，中孔直径 1.57 厘米，厚 0.79 厘米

内蒙古自治区文物考古研究院藏

Jade *Bi* (disc)

Hamin Culture (ca. 6,000–5,000 BP)

Unearthed from House Remains No. 46, Hamin Mangha Site, Horqin Left Wing Middle Banner,
Tongliao, Inner Mongolia between 2010 and 2012

Length 7.45 cm, width 6.32 cm, diameter of central hole 1.57 cm, thickness 0.79 cm

Inner Mongolia Institute of Cultural Relics and Archaeology

透闪石质，灰绿色，边缘有黑色玉皮。圆角方形玉璧。中间有一圆形钻孔，刃状边较厚，上部近外缘钻有两个小孔。坠孔上有悬挂痕迹。

173

龙衍九州
The Dragon Hovers
over China

龙腾中国：红山文化古国文明
Legends of Dragon：
The Ancient Civilization of Hongshan Culture

113. 钺形玉璧

红山文化（距今约 6500-5000 年）

1991 年辽宁省朝阳市建平县牛河梁遗址第二地点一号冢 23 号墓出土（N2Z1M23：2）

长 12.4 厘米，最宽 10.5 厘米，小孔径 0.4 厘米，厚 0.6 厘米

辽宁省文物考古研究院藏

Jade *Bi* (disc) in the shape of *Yue* (axe)

Hongshan Culture (ca. 6,500–5,000 BP)

Unearthed from Tomb No. 23, Stone Mound No. 1, Locus No. 2, Niuheliang Site, Jianping, Chaoyang, Liaoning in 1991 (N2Z1M23:2)

Length 12.4 cm, greatest width 10.5 cm, diameter of smaller hole 0.4 cm, thickness 0.6 cm

Liaoning Provincial Institute of Cultural Relics and Archaeology

　　淡青色玉质，有片状瑕疵，表层大部分钙化泛白，背面有土渍痕。形似玉钺，扁平片状体，缘部均较圆钝，其中一边为弧形，较厚，其他三边为直刃，较薄。中心有一直径 3.1 厘米的圆孔。与弧刃相对应的直边近缘部居中位置穿有双小孔，孔间磨有系沟。

114. 玉璧

红山文化（距今约 6500-5000 年）

1989 年辽宁省朝阳市建平县牛河梁遗址第二地点一号冢 21 号墓出土（N2Z1M21:9）

最大径 12.0 厘米，孔径 3.9 厘米，厚 0.6 厘米

辽宁省文物考古研究院藏

Jade *Bi* (disc)

Hongshan Culture (ca. 6,500–5,000 BP)

Unearthed from Tomb No. 21, Stone Mound No. 1, Locus No. 2, Niuheliang Site, Jianping, Chaoyang, Liaoning in 1989 (N2Z1M21:9)

Greatest diameter 12.0 cm, diameter of hole 3.9 cm, thickness 0.6 cm

Liaoning Provincial Institute of Cultural Relics and Archaeology

碧绿色。玉质匀，有白色瑕斑，瑕斑处可见原玉料凹坑。磨制光滑。外观近似圆角方形，缘部有一残缺口，内孔较圆，边缘薄锐而中部较厚，璧上端钻三小孔，左右二孔为对钻，中一孔为单钻，且孔缘有片状破损，疑似为中孔制作失误而补双孔制作。

175

龙衍九州
The Dragon Hovers
over China

龙腾中国：红山文化古国文明
Legends of Dragon：
The Ancient Civilization of Hongshan Culture

115. 玉璧

红山文化（距今约 6500-5000 年）

辽宁省朝阳市凌源市田家沟墓地 4 号墓出土（M4∶2）

长径 7.4 厘米，短径 4.8 厘米，厚 0.3 厘米

辽宁省文物考古研究院藏

Jade *Bi* (disc)

Hongshan Culture (ca. 6,500–5,000 BP)

Unearthed from Tomb No. 4, Tianjiagou Cemetery, Lingyuan, Chaoyang, Liaoning (M4:2)

Longer diameter 7.4 cm, shorter diameter 4.8 cm, thickness 0.3 cm

Liaoning Provincial Institute of Cultural Relics and Archaeology

淡黄绿色。长圆形，内外缘磨薄，内缘稍厚，体中部厚而圆鼓，上边缘钻一孔。

176

龙 衍 九 州

The Dragon Hovers
over China

『 何 以 中 国 』 文 物 考 古 大 展 系 列

"The Essence of China:" an Exhibition Series
of Cultural Relics and Archaeological Achievements

116. 方形玉璧

红山文化（距今约 6500-5000 年）

2001 年内蒙古自治区赤峰市敖汉旗草帽山遗址出土
高 9.3 厘米，上边宽 9.8 厘米，下边宽 9.4 厘米，中孔径 3.7-4.0 厘米，缘孔径 0.2 厘米，厚 0.5-0.7 厘米
敖汉博物馆（敖汉旗文物保护中心）藏

Square Jade *Bi* (disc)

Hongshan Culture (ca. 6,500–5,000 BP)

Unearthed from the Caomaoshan Site, Aohan Banner, Chifeng, Inner Mongolia in 2001

Height 9.3 cm, width of upper side 9.8 cm, width of lower side 9.4 cm, diameter of central hole 3.7–4.0 cm,

diameter of marginal hole 0.2 cm, thickness 0.5–0.7 cm

Aohan Museum (Aohan Banner Conservation Center of Cultural Relics)

　　白色玉，属鸡骨白，表面有土侵黑灰色斑点，质地细腻不透光，磨制光滑。方形，中间厚，
边缘薄，中心大圆孔为单面钻。上边缘居中钻一小圆孔，对钻而成。

117. 玉双连璧

红山文化（距今约 6500-5000 年）

2014-2016 年辽宁省朝阳市半拉山墓地 23 号墓出土（M23:1）

长 8.21 厘米，宽 3.08 厘米，厚 0.28 厘米

辽宁省文物考古研究院藏

Interconnected Double Jade *Bi* (disc)

Hongshan Culture (ca. 6,500–5,000 BP)

Unearthed from Tomb No. 23, Banlashan Cemetery, Chaoyang, Liaoning between 2014 and 2016 (M23:1)

Length 8.21 cm, width 3.08 cm, thickness 0.28 cm

Liaoning Provincial Institute of Cultural Relics and Archaeology

青绿色透闪石玉，上部有三道白色自然纹理，质地细腻通透。平面近椭圆，似鱼形，中部两侧边缘内收，将璧体分成上下两部分，似二璧相连。顶部呈圆弧状凸出，穿一细孔，作为系挂之用，底部似鱼尾形，边缘上刻出三道凹口。体扁平、轻薄，边缘薄如刃。顶部和璧心孔均为对钻而成，近圆形。通体磨制光滑。

118. 玉双连璧

红山文化（距今约 6500-5000 年）

2014-2016 年辽宁省朝阳市半拉山墓地 62 号墓出土（M62:1）

长 8.96 厘米，宽 5.37 厘米，厚 0.35 厘米

辽宁省文物考古研究院藏

Interconnected Double Jade *Bi* (disc)

Hongshan Culture (ca. 6,500–5,000 BP)

Unearthed from Tomb No. 62, Banlashan Cemetery, Chaoyang, Liaoning between 2014 and 2016 (M62:1)

Length 8.96 cm, width 5.37 cm, thickness 0.35 cm

Liaoning Provincial Institute of Cultural Relics and Archaeology

乳白色玉石质，质地较细密，器表光滑。
平面近圆角长方形，璧体扁平、轻薄，中部稍厚，
外边缘薄如刃，一侧面较平整，一侧面略呈弧形。
在两端各打磨出一孔，孔均近似圆角三角形。

119. 玉双连璧

红山文化（距今约 6500-5000 年）

2002 年辽宁省朝阳市凌源市牛河梁遗址第十六地点 1 号墓出土（N16M1:2）
长 9.1 厘米，宽 5.6 厘米，上孔径 1.3 厘米，下孔径 2.0 厘米，厚 0.4 厘米
辽宁省文物考古研究院藏

Interconnected Double Jade *Bi* (disc)

Hongshan Culture (ca. 6,500–5,000 BP)

Unearthed from Tomb No. 1, Locus No. 16, Niuheliang Site, Lingyuan, Chaoyang, Liaoning in 2002 (N16M1:2)
Length 9.1 cm, width 5.6 cm, diameter of upper hole 1.3 cm, diameter of lower hole 2.0 cm, thickness 0.4 cm
Liaoning Provincial Institute of Cultural Relics and Archaeology

绿色玉质，有一道裂纹，磨光，略显光泽，表面附着有土渍痕。器体扁薄，平面近于梯形，两侧边似一条弧线，中间以"V"形刻槽分区两璧，形成双璧相连状，上璧小而下璧大。上璧呈三角形，下璧呈方圆形，内孔均呈不规则圆形，内、外侧边缘磨薄似刃状。

120. 玉双连璧

红山文化（距今约 6500-5000 年）

1989 年辽宁省朝阳市建平县牛河梁遗址第二地点一号冢 21 号墓出土
N2Z1M21：6　长 5.5 厘米，最宽 4.7 厘米，厚 0.3 厘米
N2Z1M21：7　长 6.1 厘米，最宽 4.9 厘米，厚 0.3 厘米
辽宁省文物考古研究院藏

Interconnected Double Jade *Bi* (discs)

Hongshan Culture (ca. 6,500–5,000 BP)

Unearthed from Tomb No. 21, Stone Mound No.1, Locus No. 2, Niuheliang Site, Jianping, Chaoyang, Liaoning in 1989
N2Z1M21:6: Length 5.5 cm, greatest width 4.7 cm, thickness 0.3 cm
N2Z1M21:7: Length 6.1 cm, greatest width 4.9 cm, thickness 0.3 cm
Liaoning Provincial Institute of Cultural Relics and Archaeology

　　呈 "8" 字形。一件为绿色，有淡褐色斑痕，遗有原玉料凹点坑。顶尖圆。璧孔均为两面对钻，下孔较圆。一件淡绿色玉，泛黄，有凹坑点。上下璧孔皆不够规则。

181

龙　衍　九　州
The Dragon Hovers
over China

龙腾中国：红山文化古国文明
Legends of Dragon :
The Ancient Civilization of Hongshan Culture

121. 玉三连璧

红山文化（距今约 6500-5000 年）

2014-2016 年辽宁省朝阳市半拉山墓地 39 号墓出土（M39:3）
长 9.0 厘米，宽 4.2 厘米，孔径 1.4-1.5 厘米，厚 0.34 厘米
辽宁省文物考古研究院藏

Interconnected Triple Jade *Bi* (disc)

Hongshan Culture (ca. 6,500–5,000 BP)

Unearthed from Tomb No. 39, Banlashan Cemetery, Chaoyang, Liaoning between 2014 and 2016 (M39:3)
Length 9.0 cm, width 4.2 cm, diameter of hole 1.4–1.5 cm, thickness 0.34 cm
Liaoning Provincial Institute of Cultural Relics and Archaeology

龙衍九州
The Dragon Hovers
over China

『何以中国』文物考古大展系列
"The Essence of China:" an Exhibition Series
of Cultural Relics and Archaeological Achievements

青色玉石质，略有糖色，表面有灰白色片絮状沁，质地细腻莹润。体扁平、轻薄，整体平面近椭圆形，形似三璧相连。边缘薄似刃，横截面近梭形。体中部对钻三个形制不规则、大小不一的近圆形内孔。磨制精细，表面光滑。

122. 玉三连璧

哈民文化（距今约 6000-5000 年）

2010-2012 年内蒙古自治区通辽市科尔沁左翼中旗哈民忙哈遗址 72 号房址出土

长 7.3 厘米，宽 3.5 厘米

内蒙古自治区文物考古研究院藏

Interconnected Triple Jade *Bi* (disc)

Hamin Culture (ca. 6,000–5,000 BP)

Unearthed from House Remains No. 72, Hamin Mangha Site, Horqin Left Wing Middle Banner,

Tongliao, Inner Mongolia between 2010 and 2012

Length 7.3 cm, width 3.5 cm

Inner Mongolia Institute of Cultural Relics and Archaeology

玉质微透明，青色中大面积泛白。连璧为不规则的长条形，中间均有孔，孔的大小不一，通体磨光，光素无纹，边缘略薄，孔呈圆形。

183

龙　衍　九　州
The Dragon Hovers
over China

龙腾中国：红山文化古国文明
Legends of Dragon：
The Ancient Civilization of Hongshan Culture

123. 玉环

红山文化（距今约 6500-5000 年）

2014-2016 年辽宁省朝阳市半拉山墓地出土（T0406 ③ A:3）
直径 12.6-13.1 厘米，内孔径 10.3 厘米，厚 0.5-0.8 厘米
辽宁省文物考古研究院藏

Jade Ring

Hongshan Culture (ca. 6,500–5,000 BP)

Unearthed from Banlashan Cemetery, Chaoyang, Liaoning between 2014 and 2016 (T0406 ③ A:3)
Diameter 12.6–13.1 cm, diameter of inner hole 10.3 cm, thickness 0.5–0.8 cm
Liaoning Provincial Institute of Cultural Relics and Archaeology

龙 衍 九 州
The Dragon Hovers
over China

『何以中国』文物考古大展系列
"The Essence of China," an Exhibition Series
of Cultural Relics and Archaeological Achievements

　　青色透闪石玉质，有白色纹理。平面近圆角长方形。体宽平、硕大，粗细不均，一侧面较平滑，一侧面略呈弧形，边缘薄如刃，横截面近三角形。环体有两细孔，对钻而成，近内孔一侧的部分细孔壁被内孔钻掉。推测该玉环原应为一大型玉璧，对其进行二次钻孔切割，制作了另一件玉器，此件为剩余的废料。

124. 玉镯

红山文化（距今约 6500-5000 年）

2003 年辽宁省朝阳市凌源市牛河梁遗址第十六地点 14 号墓出土

N16M14：4　直径 8.8 厘米，孔径 6.7 厘米，厚 0.88 厘米

N16M14：7　直径 7.35 厘米，孔径 5.9 厘米，厚 0.61 厘米

辽宁省文物考古研究院藏

Jade Bracelets

Hongshan Culture (ca. 6,500–5,000 BP)

Unearthed from Tomb No. 14, Locus No. 16, Niuheliang Site, Lingyuan, Chaoyang, Liaoning in 2003

N16M14:4: Diameter 8.8 cm, diameter of hole 6.7 cm, thickness 0.88 cm

N16M14:7: Diameter 7.35 cm, diameter of hole 5.9 cm, thickness 0.61 cm

Liaoning Provincial Institute of Cultural Relics and Archaeology

　　青绿色玉质，有黑色杂质，形制规整，平面近正圆形。一件表面有土渍和灰渍。内缘两面对磨，一面磨痕较深，缘面斜平；外缘磨成圆棱，横截面近圆角三角形。近外缘处两面均见一道与镯体正切的片具开料痕。另一件断裂为四段。内、外缘渐边渐薄，磨成刃边，横截面近圆角三角形。

186

龙行九州
The Dragon Hovers
over China

『何以中国』文物考古大展系列
"The Essence of China," an Exhibition Series
of Cultural Relics and Archaeological Achievements

125. 玉镯

红山文化（距今约 6500-5000 年）

2009 年辽宁省朝阳市凌源市田家沟墓地 1 号墓、5 号墓出土
M1:1　外径 7.9 厘米，内径 6.0 厘米，厚 0.9 厘米
M5:2　外径 8.1 厘米，内径 6.1 厘米，厚 0.8 厘米
辽宁省文物考古研究院藏

Jade Bracelets

Hongshan Culture (ca. 6,500–5,000 BP)

Unearthed from Tomb No. 1 and Tomb No. 5, Tianjiagou Cemetery, Lingyuan, Chaoyang, Liaoning in 2009
M1:1: Outer diameter 7.9 cm, inner diameter 6.0 cm, thickness 0.9 cm
M5:2: Outer diameter 8.1 cm, inner diameter 6.1 cm, thickness 0.8 cm
Liaoning Provincial Institute of Cultural Relics and Archaeology

　　青绿色透闪石软玉，内有黑色杂质，器表泛白，有多处细小自然绺裂。平面近正圆形，横截面呈圆三角形。外缘磨薄，中孔内缘较厚，壁面较平。通体抛光。一件表面附着零星坚固埋藏土，另一件局部有土沁。

126. 玉锛

兴隆洼文化（距今约 8000-7000 年）

1986-1994 年辽宁省阜新市查海遗址出土

T0609　长 4.2 厘米，刃宽 2.8 厘米，厚 0.9 厘米

94FCⅠT411H34　残长 3.98 厘米，宽 0.7-0.87 厘米，厚 0.68 厘米

辽宁省文物考古研究院藏

Jade Adzes

Xinglongwa Culture (ca. 8,000–7,000 BP)

Unearthed from the Chahai Site, Fuxin, Liaoning between 1986 and 1994

T0609: Length 4.2 cm, width of blade 2.8 cm, thickness 0.9 cm

94FCⅠT411H34: Length (remaining) 3.98 cm, width 0.7–0.87 cm, thickness 0.68 cm

Liaoning Provincial Institute of Cultural Relics and Archaeology

　　一件为乳白色玉石质，磨制，平面近梯形，上端残破，有崩疤，弧刃正锋。另一件为浅绿色玉石质，通体磨制光滑，顶端有崩痕，斜直刃。

187

龙 衍 九 州
The Dragon Hovers
over China

龙腾中国：红山文化古国文明
Legends of Dragon：
The Ancient Civilization of Hongshan Culture

127. 玉斧

红山文化（距今约 6500-5000 年）

2014-2016 年辽宁省朝阳市半拉山墓地 13 号墓出土（M13:1）
长 18.9 厘米，顶宽 5.8 厘米，刃宽 7.6 厘米，厚 2.3 厘米
辽宁省文物考古研究院藏

Jade Axe

Hongshan Culture (ca. 6,500–5,000 BP)

Unearthed from Tomb No. 13, Banlashan Cemetery, Chaoyang, Liaoning between 2014 and 2016 (M13:1)
Length 18.9 cm, width of top 5.8 cm, width of blade 7.6 cm, thickness 2.3 cm
Liaoning Provincial Institute of Cultural Relics and Archaeology

188

龙 衍 九 州
The Dragon Hovers
over China

『 何 以 中 国 』 文 物 考 古 大 展 系 列
"The Essence of China," an Exhibition Series
of Cultural Relics and Archaeological Achievements

墨绿色透闪石玉，一侧面有大面积灰白色沁，质地细腻温润。整体磨制而成，形制较规整，平面近梯形，扁体，表面大部分较光滑。弧顶，一侧劈裂，劈裂面未经打磨。体两侧切割错位，未打磨平，保留错切形成的凸棱。双面弧刃，刃锋利，有使用的细小疤痕。

128. 玉铲

红山文化（距今约 6500-5000 年）

2011 年辽宁省朝阳市凌源市田家沟墓地 8 号墓出土（M8:1）

长 15.7 厘米，最宽 6.3 厘米，厚 1.0 厘米

辽宁省文物考古研究院藏

Jade Shovel

Hongshan Culture (ca. 6,500–5,000 BP)

Unearthed from Tomb No. 8, Tianjiagou Cemetery, Lingyuan, Chaoyang, Liaoning in 2011 (M8:1)

Length 15.7 cm, greatest width 6.3 cm, thickness 1.0 cm

Liaoning Provincial Institute of Cultural Relics and Archaeology

龙 衍 九 州
The Dragon Hovers
over China

龙腾中国：红山文化古国文明
Legends of Dragon：
The Ancient Civilization of Hongshan Culture

　　墨绿色透闪石玉，一面附着较厚埋藏土。铲略残损，经二次加工成器，通体抛光。器体上窄下宽，平面近三角形，较薄，单面刃，偏锋。

129. 玉斧

红山文化（距今约 6500-5000 年）

内蒙古自治区赤峰市敖汉旗北泡子沿出土
长 19.0 厘米，最宽 7.0 厘米，厚 1.7 厘米
敖汉博物馆（敖汉旗文物保护中心）藏

Jade Axe

Hongshan Culture (ca. 6,500–5,000 BP)

Unearthed from Northern Paoziyan, Aohan Banner, Chifeng, Inner Mongolia

Length 19.0 cm, greatest width 7.0 cm, thickness 1.7 cm

Aohan Museum (Aohan Banner Conservation Center of Cultural Relics)

浅绿色玉，含白色絮状物和黄、褐斑点，通体磨光。扁平体，上窄下宽，内端圆弧较薄，两侧边略外弧，弧刃较钝，刃一侧磨平，近刃部两侧有斜向使用痕迹。

『何以中国』文物考古大展系列　"The Essence of China," an Exhibition Series of Cultural Relics and Archaeological Achievements

130. 玉斧

红山文化（距今约 6500-5000 年）

内蒙古自治区赤峰市建昌营出土

长 14.0 厘米，宽 6.6 厘米

赤峰博物院藏

Jade Axe

Hongshan Culture (ca. 6,500–5,000 BP)

Unearthed from Jianchangying, Chifeng, Inner Mongolia

Length 14.0 cm, width 6.6 cm

Chifeng Museum

青玉质打磨而成，刃部较宽，玉质较差。

191

龙衍九州
The Dragon Hovers
over China

龙腾中国：红山文化古国文明
Legends of Dragon：
The Ancient Civilization of Hongshan Culture

131. 玉棒

红山文化（距今约 6500-5000 年）

内蒙古自治区赤峰市敖汉旗征集

长 29.0 厘米

内蒙古博物院藏

Jade Rod

Hongshan Culture (ca. 6,500–5,000 BP)

Acquired from Aohan Banner, Chifeng, Inner Mongolia

Length 29.0 cm

Inner Mongolia Museum

龙 衍 九 州

The Dragon Hovers
over China

『何 以 中 国』 文 物 考 古 大 展 系 列

"The Essence of China," an Exhibition Series
of Cultural Relics and Archaeological Achievements

　　优质透闪石，整体呈湖绿色，有黑色斑点，玉料应来自贝加尔湖地区。器形中间起鼓，两边往末端逐渐收成钝尖状，一端圆尖，另一端略平。器表为多面成圆，打磨痕迹明显，局部有牙黄色沁。整体幽光内敛，抛光精湛，为这一时期较少见的礼器类型。

132. 联珠形玉饰件

红山文化（距今约 6500-5000 年）

内蒙古自治区赤峰市翁牛特旗半砬山出土

长 9.8 厘米，宽 1.1-1.7 厘米

赤峰博物院藏

Beading-shaped Jade Ornament

Hongshan Culture (ca. 6,500–5,000 BP)

Unearthed from Banlashan, Ongniud Banner, Chifeng, Inner Mongolia

Length 9.8 cm, width 1.1–1.7 cm

Chifeng Museum

193

龙衍九州
The Dragon Hovers
over China

龙腾中国：红山文化古国文明
Legends of Dragon :
The Ancient Civilization of Hongshan Culture

青绿色玉质，饰件呈柱状六节联珠形，上部一侧有一短钩。

133. "印章形" 玉器

红山文化（距今约 6500-5000 年）

1984 年辽宁省朝阳市建平县牛河梁遗址第二地点四号冢 1 号灰坑出土（N2Z4H1∶15）
高 3.4 厘米，底边宽 0.55-1.0 厘米，体宽 0.5-1.1 厘米，厚 0.25-0.35 厘米
辽宁省文物考古研究院藏

Seal-shaped Jade Object

Hongshan Culture (ca. 6,500–5,000 BP)

Unearthed from Ash Pit No. 1, Stone Mound No. 4, Locus No. 2, Niuheliang Site, Jianping, Chaoyang, Liaoning in 1984 (N2Z4H1:15)
Height 3.4 cm, width of base 0.55–1.0 cm, width of body 0.5–1.1 cm, thickness 0.25–0.35 cm
Liaoning Provincial Institute of Cultural Relics and Archaeology

194

龙 衍 九 州

The Dragon Hovers
over China

『 何 以 中 国 』 文 物 考 古 大 展 系 列

"The Essence of China," an Exhibition Series
of Cultural Relics and Archaeological Achievements

　　黑色滑石质。体小而规整，磨制，表面光滑，两侧各显数道划线痕。有长方形底座，略呈梯形器体和三凸形冠状饰，顶部与器体之间起一甚细的纽带状凸棱间隔，总体形似一印章。

134. 玉杖头

红山文化（距今约 6500-5000 年）

2014-2016 年辽宁省朝阳市半拉山墓地出土（T0507 ③ A：1）
高 3.62 厘米，上端长径 5.25 厘米、短径 4.12 厘米，下端直径 3.55 厘米，粗孔径 3.11 厘米，孔深 2.7 厘米
辽宁省文物考古研究院藏

Jade Staff Head

Hongshan Culture (ca. 6,500–5,000 BP)

Unearthed from Banlashan Cemetery, Chaoyang, Liaoning between 2014 and 2016 (T0507 ③ A:1)
Height 3.62 cm, longer diameter of upper part 5.25 cm, shorter diameter of upper part 4.12 cm, diameter of lower part 3.55 cm, diameter of bigger hole 3.11 cm, depth of hole 2.7 cm
Liaoning Provincial Institute of Cultural Relics and Archaeology

　　乳白色玉石质，表面有黑黄色沁。形制规整，整体呈倒梯形台体，顶面宽大，平面为椭圆形，钻有两个小孔，一孔为双面对钻，对钻略有错位，一孔为单面钻。底面窄小，平面近圆形。单面钻一粗大深孔，孔口粗，孔底变细呈圜底状，与两细孔相通。

195

龙　衍　九　州
The Dragon Hovers
over China

龙腾中国：红山文化古国文明
Legends of Dragon：
The Ancient Civilization of Hongshan Culture

135. 玉管钻芯

红山文化（距今约 6500-5000 年）

2014 年辽宁省朝阳市半拉山墓地 20 号墓出土（M20：7）

长 3.89 厘米，宽 3.71 厘米，厚 1.65 厘米

辽宁省文物考古研究院藏

Jade Core Gouged out with a Tubular Drill

Hongshan Culture (ca. 6,500–5,000 BP)

Unearthed from Tomb No. 20, Banlashan Cemetery, Chaoyang, Liaoning in 2014 (M20:7)

Length 3.89 cm, width 3.71 cm, thickness 1.65 cm

Liaoning Provincial Institute of Cultural Relics and Archaeology

『何以中国』文物考古大展系列

"The Essence of China," an Exhibition Series
of Cultural Relics and Archaeological Achievements

绿色。扁圆柱形，截面呈圆形，中部有对钻痕迹，呈两段状。

136. 玉管钻芯

红山文化（距今约 6500-5000 年）

2014 年辽宁省朝阳市半拉山墓地 20 号墓出土（M20:15）
通高 6.0 厘米，最大径 9.3 厘米，芯高 2.6 厘米，芯径 4.8 厘米
辽宁省文物考古研究院藏

Jade Core Gouged out with a Tubular Drill

Hongshan Culture (ca. 6,500–5,000 BP)

Unearthed from Tomb No. 20, Banlashan Cemetery, Chaoyang, Liaoning in 2014 (M20:15)

Overall height 6.0 cm, greatest diameter 9.3 cm, height of core 2.6 cm, diameter of core 4.8 cm

Liaoning Provincial Institute of Cultural Relics and Archaeology

绿色。圆柱状，中部有管钻痕迹。

197

龙　衍　九　州
The Dragon Hovers
over China

龙腾中国：红山文化古国文明
Legends of Dragon :
The Ancient Civilization of Hongshan Culture

　　红山文化发达的动物题材玉器植根于西辽河流域渔猎文化传统，直观反映了红山文化先民万物有灵和动物崇拜观念，鸟、兽、龟、鱼、虫等类型玉器造型生动，充满灵性，成为红山文化玉礼器系统的重要内容。

137. 龙凤玉佩

红山文化（距今约 6500-5000 年）

1991 年辽宁省朝阳市建平县牛河梁遗址第二地点一号冢 23 号墓出土（N2Z1M23：3）

长 10.3 厘米，宽 7.8 厘米，厚 0.9 厘米

辽宁省文物考古研究院藏

198

龙衍九州
The Dragon Hovers
over China

『何以中国』文物考古大展系列
"The Essence of China," an Exhibition Series
of Cultural Relics and Archaeological Achievements

Dragon-and-phoenix-shaped Jade Pendant

Hongshan Culture (ca. 6,500–5,000 BP)

Unearthed from Tomb No. 23, Stone Mound No.1, Locus No. 2, Niuheliang Site, Jianping, Chaoyang, Liaoning in 1991 (N2Z1M23:3)

Length 10.3 cm, width 7.8 cm, thickness 0.9 cm

Liaoning Provincial Institute of Cultural Relics and Archaeology

　　长方形，长边两侧有红褐色间白色瑕斑，应为原玉料的皮壳部分所遗。呈板状，较厚，稍向背面内弯。有正、背面之分，正面以减地阳纹与较粗的阴线雕出一龙一凤，都以头部雕刻为主，身体简化。横置可见一龙首，圆目较鼓，吻长，吻端圆而有上翘，有圆窝状鼻孔，额与吻边饰表现皮毛的短阴线，顶后部有斜长突尖为双角，龙体作外卷。立置又见一凤鸟，勾啄尖锐，圆目外鼓，顶冠以短阴线表现羽毛，背有下垂状的三尖突，似为凤鸟长羽，体亦外卷，与龙体相对相接。反面平而无纹。龙凤之间以一桃形孔相隔，龙凤身体卷曲而成孔均为两面对钻。背面另有 3 组隧孔，或可系戴。

138. 双龙首玉璜

红山文化（距今约 6500-5000 年）

1979-1982 年辽宁省朝阳市喀左县东山嘴遗址出土

长 4.1 厘米

辽宁省博物馆藏

Jade *Huang* (arc-shaped pendant) with Dragon-head-shaped Carvings Flanking on Both Sides

Hongshan Culture (ca. 6,500–5,000 BP)

Unearthed from the Dongshanzui Site, Kazuo, Chaoyang, Liaoning between 1979 and 1982

Length 4.1 cm

Liaoning Provincial Museum

　　该玉璜以青玉为原料，玉质晶莹润泽，坚硬细腻。玉璜呈半圆形，两端对称分布龙首。龙吻上扬呈卷曲状，瞠目张口的神态极具震慑力。龙身以浅浮雕结合阴刻线工艺表现起伏的躯体，边缘打磨薄锐，谷纹、云纹等辅助纹饰均匀饱满，体现红山文化晚期制玉技术的高度成熟。龙体中部相连，构成"双龙共体"的抽象造型，兼具写实与象征意义，推测其可能与祭祀仪式中的神权象征相关。作为红山文化首件考古发掘的龙形玉器，其双龙首造型印证了辽河流域早期龙崇拜的独特性。

　　东山嘴双龙首玉璜以青玉材质、精湛工艺与独特双龙造型，成为红山文化玉器中的典范。其设计融合实用性与宗教象征，既是身份标识，又是沟通天地的媒介，为研究中华早期文明形态提供了关键性的实物依据。

红山文化（距今约 6500–5000 年）

1987 年辽宁省朝阳市建平县牛河梁遗址第二地点一号冢出土（N2Z1:C8）

长 3.1 厘米，最厚 0.7 厘米

辽宁省文物考古研究院藏

Jade Phoenix Head

Hongshan Culture (ca. 6,500–5,000 BP)

Unearthed from Stone Mound No.1, Locus No. 2, Niuheliang Site, Jianping, Chaoyang, Liaoning in 1987 (N2Z1:C8)

Length 3.1 cm, greatest thickness 0.7 cm

Liaoning Provincial Institute of Cultural Relics and Archaeology

龙 衍 九 州

The Dragon Hovers
over China

『何 以 中 国』文 物 考 古 大 展 系 列

"The Essence of China," an Exhibition Series
of Cultural Relics and Archaeological Achievements

　　滑石质，淡黄色，表皮间深褐色。形小，片状。正面以较粗的阴线雕出如钩的喙弯，臣字目，目四周阴刻波状，斜线或直线，头顶以扉棱作其冠羽，延至头后部。背面磨平，背面中部有穿孔。

140. 双兽（鸮）首玉佩

红山文化（距今约 6500-5000 年）

1991 年辽宁省朝阳市建平县牛河梁遗址第二地点一号冢 26 号墓出土（N2Z1M26:2）

长 12.9 厘米，宽 9.5 厘米，厚 0.6 厘米

辽宁省文物考古研究院藏

Double-animal (owl)-shaped Jade Pendant

Hongshan Culture (ca. 6,500–5,000 BP)

Unearthed from Tomb No. 26, Stone Mound No.1, Locus No. 2, Niuheliang Site, Jianping, Chaoyang, Liaoning in 1991 (N2Z1M26:2)

Length 12.9 cm, width 9.5 cm, thickness 0.6 cm

Liaoning Provincial Institute of Cultural Relics and Archaeology

　　板状体，边缘磨薄。有正、背面之分。正面两端各雕一兽首，上下对称。兽首有立耳，额中起突尖，耳端圆而不起尖，目椭圆状，嘴部由两侧向下延伸，嘴端圆。似兽似鸮。中部镂空，两侧以起地法各作出六道瓦沟纹，外侧缘又各作出三个突起的扉棱，一侧的上部扉棱边缘并钻半孔。背无纹饰，有三组呈品字状布局的隧孔，用于穿系。

141. 兽面玉牌饰

红山文化（距今约 6500-5000 年）

1989 年辽宁省朝阳市建平县牛河梁遗址第二地点一号冢 21 号墓出土（N2Z1M21：14）

通高 10.2 厘米，最阔 14.7 厘米，厚 0.4 厘米

辽宁省文物考古研究院藏

Jade Plaque Ornament with Animal-mask Pattern

Hongshan Culture (ca. 6,500–5,000 BP)

Unearthed from Tomb No. 21, Stone Mound No.1, Locus No. 2, Niuheliang Site, Jianping, Chaoyang, Liaoning in 1989 (N2Z1M21:14)

Overall height 10.2 cm, greatest width 14.7 cm, thickness 0.4 cm

Liaoning Provincial Institute of Cultural Relics and Archaeology

龙 衍 九 州
The Dragon Hovers
over China

『何 以 中 国』文 物 考 古 大 展 系 列
"The Essence of China," an Exhibition Series
of Cultural Relics and Archaeological Achievements

　　淡绿色玉质。通体磨平，体薄而两面都甚为平整，两面都雕出兽首形象。双耳长而竖起，耳端起尖。钻孔表现圆目及鼻孔，目孔以一面钻为主，一目孔缘斜直，以阴线刻出耳根端、眉际、额间皱折，以及鼻、嘴部轮廓线。此玉器整体造型对称庄重，线条简洁明快，主要特征突出。

142. 兽面丫形玉器

红山文化（距今约 6500-5000 年）

辽宁省文物总店征集

高 15.2 厘米，宽 2.8 厘米，厚 0.35 厘米

辽宁省博物馆藏

Y-shaped Jade Object with Animal-mask Pattern

Hongshan Culture (ca. 6,500–5,000 BP)

Acquired from the Liaoning Cultural Relics Flagship Store

Length 15.2 cm, width 2.8 cm, thickness 0.35 cm

Liaoning Provincial Museum

龙 衍 九 州
The Dragon Hovers
over China

『何以中国』文物考古大展系列
"The Essence of China," an Exhibition Series
of Cultural Relics and Archaeological Achievements

深绿色，中部一面有大片黄色瑕斑及裂纹。长条板状，甚为扁平。形体甚细长，首部刻纹已不显，似为出土后长期磨损所为。圆睛不规则，短圆弧线相接成睛的作法更为明显。有对称双鼻孔。体饰弦纹较宽且较深，使两侧边缘也起与弦纹对应的棱线。近底部中央对钻单孔。

143. 兽面丫形玉器

红山文化（距今约 6500-5000 年）

辽宁省文物总店征集

高 9.5 厘米，宽 3.1 厘米

辽宁省博物馆藏

Y-shaped Jade Object with Animal-mask Pattern

Hongshan Culture (ca. 6,500–5,000 BP)

Acquired by the Liaoning Cultural Relics Flagship Store

Length 9.5 cm, width 3.1 cm

Liaoning Provincial Museum

淡绿色。长方形板状。上部雕兽面纹，双耳上竖，与头部呈"丫"字形。头部以细阴线雕琢大圆眼和面部褶皱，眼下钻两小孔为鼻孔。宽嘴，嘴角突出体外，以嘴为头与身体（器柄）的分界。柄部用打磨减地技法，琢磨出十余道凸凹相间的横弦纹。器物下端钻一小孔，残缺一角。

144. 玉兽首

红山文化（距今约 6500-5000 年）

高 3.5 厘米，宽 4.5 厘米

天津博物馆藏

Jade Animal Head

Hongshan Culture (ca. 6,500–5,000 BP)

Height 3.5 cm, width 4.5 cm

Tianjin Museum

龙衍九州

The Dragon Hovers
over China

『何以中国』文物考古大展系列

"The Essence of China," an Exhibition Series
of Cultural Relics and Archaeological Achievements

　　玉质浅绿色。圆雕，首上端有圆弧形双立耳，吻部上翘前凸，正面有圆形鼻孔，鼻梁琢磨数道浅阳线表现褶皱，器中部对钻一孔以示双眼，短榫为颈。

145. 双人首三孔玉梳背饰

红山文化（距今约 6500-5000 年）

1987 年辽宁省朝阳市建平县牛河梁遗址第二地点一号冢 17 号墓出土（N2Z1M17：1）

长 6.8 厘米，最宽 3.1 厘米，大孔径 1.5 厘米，厚 0.6 厘米

辽宁省文物考古研究院藏

Jade Comb Shaft Ornament with Human-head-shaped Carvings Flanking on Both Sides and Three Holes

Hongshan Culture (ca. 6,500–5,000 BP)

Unearthed from Tomb No. 17, Stone Mound No.1, Locus No. 2, Niuheliang Site, Jianping, Chaoyang, Liaoning in 1987 (N2Z1M17:1)

Length 6.8 cm, greatest width 3.1 cm, diameter of bigger hole 1.5 cm, thickness 0.6 cm

Liaoning Provincial Institute of Cultural Relics and Archaeology

　　通体磨光。两面对称雕刻。器身两端各雕一人首，有冠，额前突，面部略凹，圆目，鼻较大，鼻头圆，口微张，下颌略长，颌端稍有外突。器体中间对钻大小相同、等距排列的三个较大圆孔，底部较薄，应为榫部，榫面对钻三个细小系孔。两排孔之间凸起一宽棱，上阴刻短斜线为饰。

208

龙衍九州
The Dragon Hovers
over China

『何以中国』文物考古大展系列
"The Essence of China:" an Exhibition Series
of Cultural Relics and Archaeological Achievements

146. 双兽首三孔玉梳背饰

红山文化（距今约 6500-5000 年）

1979 年辽宁省朝阳市凌源市牛河梁遗址第十六地点 1 号墓出土（N16-79M1）
长 8.9 厘米，宽 2.6 厘米，圆孔直径 1.9 厘米
辽宁省博物馆藏

Jade Comb Shaft Ornament with Animal-head-shaped Carvings Flanking on Both Sides and Three Holes

Hongshan Culture (ca. 6,500–5,000 BP)

Unearthed from Tomb No. 1, Locus No. 16, Niuheliang Site, Lingyuan, Chaoyang, Liaoning in 1979 (N16-79M1)

Length 8.9 cm, width 2.6 cm, diameter of round hole 1.9 cm

Liaoning Provincial Museum

青白色，玉质中杂有较大面积黑色瑕斑。黑色瑕斑集中分布于两端和一面的中下部，中下部黑斑处并遗有原玉料岩面的大片凹坑痕。器体作长条状，上宽而下窄，顶部呈三联弧状，底部平直，近底缘窄如榫。两端各圆雕一兽首。兽首额顶隆起，面廓近于三角形。双耳较短，呈圆弧状斜立。吻部前突，稍有上翘。眼眶用减地凸起的菱形表示，眶中各用一道阴刻线表现双睛。皆具熊首特征。双兽首五官细部又各有不同：一兽首尖吻甚上翘，一耳较低且显内贴状；另一兽首吻端较宽，上翘不甚。器身中部并排管钻有三个较大的圆孔，底面近边缘处钻有四个与三圆孔相通的小圆孔。小圆孔每两两居于一侧，略呈漏斗形，以单面钻为主。在底座和三圆孔之间的双侧面上还阴刻一行平行短斜线纹。通体抛光。

147. 三孔玉器

红山文化（距今约 6500-5000 年）

长 7.0 厘米，宽 2.7 厘米

天津博物馆藏

Jade Object with Three Holes

Hongshan Culture (ca. 6,500–5,000 BP)

Length 7.0 cm, width 2.7 cm

Tianjin Museum

玉质浅绿色。器两端琢磨似蛇首，器身上部有大小相近的并列三孔，使上端呈三联弧形，孔下部阴刻平行的短斜线纹，下端榫部平直，依次排列对钻孔四个。

209

龙 衍 九 州
The Dragon Hovers
over China

龙腾中国：红山文化古国文明
Legends of Dragon :
The Ancient Civilization of Hongshan Culture

148. 玉蝉

兴隆洼文化（距今约 8000-7000 年）

1988-1991 年内蒙古自治区赤峰市林西县白音长汗遗址 7 号墓出土
长 3.55 厘米，宽 1.2 厘米，厚 1.1 厘米
内蒙古自治区文物考古研究院藏

Jade Cicada

Xinglongwa Culture (ca. 8,000–7,000 BP)

Unearthed from Tomb No. 7, Baiyinchanghan Site, Linxi, Chifeng, Inner Mongolia between 1988 and 1991
Length 3.55 cm, width 1.2 cm, thickness 1.1 cm
Inner Mongolia Institute of Cultural Relics and Archaeology

黄绿色玉。磨制精细，光滑。圆雕，器表上有自然裂隙纹理。弧背，头前部顶上有一浅凹槽，头前部底下有两个竖向凹槽，呈八字形，两侧各有一个横向凹槽。向下有两道横凹槽，之下内凹，腹部有四道凹槽。头部有一个横向圆形钻孔，两面对钻。

149. 玉蚕

红山文化（距今约 6500–5000 年）

辽宁省朝阳市凌源市牛河梁遗址第五地点一号冢出土（N5SCZ1:3）

长 6.1 厘米

辽宁省文物考古研究院藏

Jade Silkworm

Hongshan Culture (ca. 6,500–5,000 BP)

Unearthed from Stone Mound No.1, Locus No. 5, Niuheliang Site, Lingyuan, Chaoyang, Liaoning (N5SCZ1:3)

Length 6.1 cm

Liaoning Provincial Institute of Cultural Relics and Archaeology

　　白色。短身，扁圆体，整体显圆而厚。似蚕蛹，头部稍长而圆鼓，头的端面磨出小平面，凹腰，腰间阴刻四道弦纹，弦纹较粗，可见接头处，尾端面平。

150. 玉蚕

红山文化（距今约 6500-5000 年）

2011 年辽宁省朝阳市凌源市田家沟墓地 3 号墓出土（M3:2）

长 6.8 厘米，宽 2.8 厘米，厚 2.0 厘米

辽宁省文物考古研究院藏

Jade Silkworm

Hongshan Culture (ca. 6,500–5,000 BP)

Unearthed from Tomb No. 3, Tianjiagou Cemetery, Lingyuan, Chaoyang, Liaoning in 2011 (M3:2)

Length 6.8 cm, width 2.8 cm, thickness 2.0 cm

Liaoning Provincial Institute of Cultural Relics and Archaeology

龙衍九州 The Dragon Hovers over China

『何以中国』文物考古大展系列 "The Essence of China," an Exhibition Series of Cultural Relics and Archaeological Achievements

透闪石软玉，鸡骨白色沁，通体抛光。器体近扁圆柱状，截面近半圆形，一面略平一面圆鼓。形似蚕，头端平，尾端斜弧收。背部平，腹部圆鼓并饰三道凸棱。

151. 玉蚕

红山文化（距今约 6500-5000 年）

1982 内蒙古自治区赤峰市巴林右旗那日斯台遗址出土

长 7.8 厘米，宽 3.4 厘米，厚 2.5 厘米

巴林右旗博物馆藏

Jade Silkworm

Hongshan Culture (ca. 6,500–5,000 BP)

Unearthed from the Narisitai Site, Bairin Right Banner, Chifeng, Inner Mongolia in 1982

Length 7.8 cm, width 3.4 cm, thickness 2.5 cm

Bairin Right Banner Museum

　　黄玉质地，略呈扁圆柱状，头端扁平，尾端尖圆，腹部微凹并横向对穿一孔。蚕首用两条细阴线纹雕琢出一双大圆眼，两眼中间有一道凸棱，凸棱下方用三角形凹槽表示嘴部。面部上方边缘有一对突出触角。蚕身腹部一面用线状阳纹表现体节。

152. 玉蚕

红山文化（距今约 6500-5000 年）

内蒙古自治区赤峰市巴林右旗境内征集

长 3.9 厘米，宽 2.1 厘米，厚 2.2 厘米

长 3.8 厘米，宽 2.1 厘米，厚 2.0 厘米

内蒙古博物院藏

Jade Silkworms

Hongshan Culture (ca. 6,500–5,000 BP)

Acquired from Bairin Right Banner, Chifeng, Inner Mongolia

Length 3.9 cm, width 2.1 cm, thickness 2.2 cm

Length 3.8 cm, width 2.1 cm, thickness 2.0 cm

Inner Mongolia Museum

　　岫岩闪石玉，黄绿色，整体表面布有云雾沁，阴刻线槽底白化显著。器形呈圆柱体，前端较粗为头部，且为椭圆形的平端面，端面中部偏下阴刻双目。目下以倒"八"字形阴刻来表现口部，蚕体前平，近尾部下弯，器表以减地阳线弦纹来表示蚕的局部特征。另一面琢有一对蝉翼，器体靠近头部两侧有一对穿孔。这种仿生玉器是红山文化先民信仰体系里重要的一种表现形式，借助玉之神力通天达地，联系神祇，以实现重生。

153. 玉蝗

红山文化（距今约 6500-5000 年）

1988 年辽宁省朝阳市凌源市牛河梁遗址第五地点二号冢 9 号墓出土（N5Z2M9∶1）

长 5.5 厘米

辽宁省文物考古研究院藏

Jade Locust

Hongshan Culture (ca. 6,500–5,000 BP)

Unearthed from Tomb No. 9, Stone Mound No. 2, Locus No. 5, Niuheliang Site, Lingyuan, Chaoyang, Liaoning in 1988 (N5Z2M9:1)

Length 5.5 cm

Liaoning Provincial Institute of Cultural Relics and Archaeology

215

龙行九州
The Dragon Hovers
over China

龙腾中国：红山文化古国文明
Legends of Dragon：
The Ancient Civilization of Hongshan Culture

  青绿色，有瑕斑。圆雕。精工雕刻出头部、面部的眼、嘴颊、双翅和下弯的腹部。身体部分仅勾勒出轮廓，无细节表现。腹下前部对钻一个穿孔。此雕件虽线条较为简略，但整体造型准确，线条简洁明快，形神兼备。

154. 玉蝈蝈

红山文化（距今约 6500-5000 年）

2003 年辽宁省朝阳市凌源市牛河梁遗址第十六地点一号冢出土（N16Z1 ① :47）

高 2.35 厘米，长 5.4 厘米，宽 1.4 厘米

辽宁省文物考古研究院藏

Jade Katydid

Hongshan Culture (ca. 6,500–5,000 BP)

Unearthed from Stone Mound No.1, Locus No. 16, Niuheliang Site, Lingyuan, Chaoyang, Liaoning in 2003 (N16Z1 ① :47)

Height 2.35 cm, length 5.4 cm, width 1.4 cm

Liaoning Provincial Institute of Cultural Relics and Archaeology

　　淡绿色玉质，绿中泛黄，一侧遗有原玉料岩面的凹坑点。通体磨光。器体圆雕，略呈长方形。头部呈长方形，上窄下宽，胸部较短，背顶用"V"形凹槽状宽线与翅膀分界，胸下用阴刻线表示前腿；腹部细长，用宽沟槽短线表现四道腹节，腹尾圆尖，略呈下垂状，腹上用锐利沟槽与磨豁技法与上扬翅膀分离，沟槽有歧出现象；翅膀呈直翅形，前翅叠压后翅，前翅狭窄而后翅较宽，作振翅欲飞状，上部正中用一道沟槽将翅膀对分左右。位于头、胸之间的沟槽深，内对穿一圆孔，管钻而成。线条虽粗简，但各部位表现得细致到位。

155. 玉鸟

红山文化（距今约 6500-5000 年）

2014 年辽宁省朝阳市半拉山墓地出土（K5：4）

长 4.0 厘米，宽 2.8 厘米

辽宁省文物考古研究院藏

Jade Bird

Hongshan Culture (ca. 6,500–5,000 BP)

Unearthed from the Banlashan Cemetery, Chaoyang, Liaoning in 2014 (K5:4)

Length 4.0 cm, width 2.8 cm

Liaoning Provincial Institute of Cultural Relics and Archaeology

绿色。鸟状，双翼展开下垂，阴刻双翼和尾部鸟羽。通体磨光。

156. 玉鸮

红山文化（距今约 6500-5000 年）

1982 年内蒙古自治区赤峰市巴林右旗那日斯台遗址出土

高 2.4 厘米，宽 3.0 厘米，厚 0.6 厘米

巴林右旗博物馆藏

Jade Owl

Hongshan Culture (ca. 6,500–5,000 BP)

Unearthed from the Narisitai Site, Bairin Right Banner, Chifeng, Inner Mongolia in 1982

Height 2.4 cm, width 3.0 cm, thickness 0.6 cm

Bairin Right Banner Museum

『何 以 中 国』文 物 考 古 大 展 系 列

"The Essence of China," an Exhibition Series
of Cultural Relics and Archaeological Achievements

　　黄玉质地，头略呈椭圆形，双眼微凸，尖嘴，翅尾舒展。背面有一对穿孔，孔下端以数道细密的阴线表现羽纹。

157. 玉鸮

红山文化（距今约 6500-5000 年）

高 4.68 厘米，宽 4.63 厘米，厚 1.24 厘米

朝阳博物馆藏

Jade Owl

Hongshan Culture (ca. 6,500–5,000 BP)

Height 4.68 cm, width 4.63 cm, thickness 1.24 cm

Chaoyang Museum

　　透闪石玉质，青黄色，表面受云雾状白沁。鸮首呈三角形，阴线打洼出圆形双眼，勾喙较短，双翅展开，以三道阴线勾勒羽翅呈展翅飞翔状。阴线刻画出长方形胸部轮廓。下方减地刻画两道斜形凸起的鸟足，尾部宽展，足部和尾部之间刻画三角形网格纹饰。背面稍内凹，头后纵向对穿一孔。整体造型生动传神，将鸟的飞翔姿态表现得淋漓尽致。

　　鸮鸟类题材玉器是红山文化的典型器，也是先民对鸟类飞翔能力的崇拜体现。

158. 玉鸮

红山文化（距今约 6500-5000 年）

高 5.3 厘米，宽 5.0 厘米

天津博物馆藏

Jade Owl

Hongshan Culture (ca. 6,500–5,000 BP)

Height 5.3 cm, width 5.0 cm

Tianjin Museum

玉质青绿色。圆雕展翅立鸮，鸮双目圆凸，喙部尖圆，肩平，双翅及尾部平展，琢磨浅阳线表现羽毛，浅浮雕双爪并紧贴腹部，背面无纹，近颈部有一组对穿孔。

159. 玉鹰

红山文化（距今约 6500-5000 年）

长 5.4 厘米，宽 4.7 厘米，厚 2.0 厘米

敖汉博物馆（敖汉旗文物保护中心）藏

Jade Eagle

Hongshan Culture (ca. 6,500–5,000 BP)

Length 5.4 cm, width 4.7 cm, thickness 2.0 cm

Aohan Museum (Aohan Banner Conservation Center of Cultural Relics)

黄色玉，有橘红色斑沁，通体抛光。圆目凸突，勾喙较短，双翅展开，双爪作下抓状，尾展开，略呈扇面状并向前卷，颈后部穿象鼻孔。

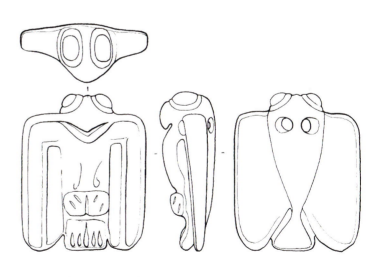

221

龙 衍 九 州
The Dragon Hovers
over China

龙腾中国：红山文化古国文明
Legends of Dragon :
The Ancient Civilization of Hongshan Culture

160. 玉蝙蝠

红山文化（距今约 6500-5000 年）

1992 年内蒙古自治区赤峰市巴林右旗查干敖包出土

长 3.8 厘米，宽 3.4 厘米，厚 0.6 厘米

巴林右旗博物馆藏

Jade Bat

Hongshan Culture (ca. 6,500–5,000 BP)

Unearthed from Chagan Obo, Bairin Right Banner, Chifeng, Inner Mongolia in 1992

Length 3.8 cm, width 3.4 cm, thickness 0.6 cm

Bairin Right Banner Museum

青玉质地，整体呈倒挂蝙蝠状，正面微鼓，阴线刻翅膀，三角形头部，大耳，椭圆形眼，嘴为一横线，上部有两条环状线，似倒挂爪，背面光洁，平整如镜。

龙衍九州
The Dragon Hovers
over China

『何以中国』文物考古大展系列
"The Essence of China," an Exhibition Series
of Cultural Relics and Archaeological Achievements

161. 绿松石鸮

红山文化（距今约 6500-5000 年）

1979-1982 年辽宁省朝阳市喀左县东山嘴遗址出土（TC ⑥ 2:1）
高 2.4 厘米，宽 2.8 厘米，厚 0.4 厘米
辽宁省文物考古研究院藏

Turquoise Owl

Hongshan Culture (ca. 6,500–5,000 BP)

Unearthed from the Dongshanzui Site, Kazuo, Chaoyang, Liaoning between 1979 and 1982 (TC ⑥ 2:1)
Height 2.4 cm, width 2.8 cm, thickness 0.4 cm
Liaoning Provincial Institute of Cultural Relics and Archaeology

绿松石质。整体呈片状，分两层，作展翅鸮形。正面用细线雕出鸮的头部、两翼及尾部，背面附黑皮，正中对穿单孔。

223

龙 衍 九 州
The Dragon Hovers
over China

龙腾中国：红山文化古国文明
Legends of Dragon：
The Ancient Civilization of Hongshan Culture

162. 鸟形玉佩

哈民文化（距今约 6000-5000 年）

2010-2012 年内蒙古自治区通辽市科尔沁左翼中旗哈民忙哈遗址 57 号房址出土

长 6.0 厘米，宽 2.6 厘米

内蒙古自治区文物考古研究院藏

Bird-shaped Jade Pendant

Hamin Culture (ca. 6,000–5,000 BP)

Unearthed from House Remains No. 57, Hamin Mangha Site, Horqin Left Wing Middle Banner,

Tongliao, Inner Mongolia between 2010 and 2012

Length 6.0 cm, width 2.6 cm

Inner Mongolia Institute of Cultural Relics and Archaeology

　　玉佩饰表面大体呈深绿色，玉质细腻致密，器身呈鸟形。顶端带有圆形孔状，用于穿孔悬挂装饰佩戴。

224

龙衍九州

The Dragon Hovers
over China

『何以中国』文物考古大展系列

"The Essence of China," an Exhibition Series
of Cultural Relics and Archaeological Achievements

163. 碧玺鱼形坠

红山文化（距今约 6500-5000 年）

1982 年内蒙古自治区赤峰市巴林右旗那日斯台遗址出土
长 4.8 厘米，宽 1.8 厘米，厚 1.3 厘米
巴林右旗博物馆藏

Fish-shaped Tourmaline Pendant

Hongshan Culture (ca. 6,500–5,000 BP)

Unearthed from the Narisitai Site, Bairin Right Banner, Chifeng, Inner Mongolia in 1982

Length 4.8 cm, width 1.8 cm, thickness 1.3 cm

Bairin Right Banner Museum

浅绿色碧玺类石英岩质地。扁圆锥形体，颈部有一周阴刻弦纹，似为鱼腮，钻孔表现鱼眼，圆嘴呈凹坑状，左侧顺体方向刻一道沟痕，右侧刻两道沟痕似为鱼翅，尾端变细呈钝尖。

225

龙衍九州
The Dragon Hovers over China

龙腾中国：红山文化古国文明
Legends of Dragon :
The Ancient Civilization of Hongshan Culture

164. 绿松石鱼形坠

红山文化（距今约 6500-5000 年）

1973 年辽宁省阜新市胡头沟遗址出土
M3-3:1　长 2.7 厘米，宽 0.7 厘米，厚 0.2 厘米
M3-5:1　长 2.5 厘米，宽 0.8 厘米，厚 0.2 厘米
辽宁省博物馆藏

Fish-shaped Turquoise Pendants

Hongshan Culture (ca. 6,500–5,000 BP)

Unearthed from Tomb No. 3, Hutougou Site, Fuxin, Liaoning in 1973
M3-3:1: Length 2.7 cm, width 0.7 cm, thickness 0.2 cm
M3-5:1: Length 2.5 cm, width 0.8 cm, thickness 0.2 cm
Liaoning Provincial Museum

龙 衍 九 州

The Dragon Hovers
over China

『何以中国』文物考古大展系列

"The Essence of China: an Exhibition Series
of Cultural Relics and Archaeological Achievements

　　两件形制质料相同，应为一对。鱼形扁平片状，颜色绿中泛蓝。表层为绿松石质，背面有一层黑色石皮，雕有鱼鳍、尾、头，形态抽象简练。一穿孔为目，可穿系，据此推测其为耳坠。鱼形坠常与玉鸮、玉龟等动物形玉器共存，体现红山先民将自然生灵神格化的信仰体系。这种鱼形设计很可能反映了红山文化的渔猎生活或水生图腾崇拜。绿松石坠多出土于积石冢等高等级墓葬，应是贵族或祭司阶层的身份象征。绿松石的蓝色调可能被红山人赋予沟通天地的神秘意义，强化祭祀仪式的神圣性。

165. 玉贝

红山文化（距今约 6500-5000 年）

1985 年辽宁省朝阳市建平县牛河梁遗址第二地点一号冢出土（N2Z1C:3，N2Z1C:4，N2Z1C:5）
长 2.0-2.2 厘米，宽 1.4-1.8 厘米，厚 0.65-0.75 厘米
辽宁省文物考古研究院藏

Jade Shells

Hongshan Culture (ca. 6,500–5,000 BP)

Unearthed from Stone Mound No. 1, Locus No. 2, Niuheliang Site, Jianping, Chaoyang, Liaoning in 1985 (N2Z1C:3, N2Z1C:4, N2Z1C:5)

Length 2.0-2.2 cm, width 1.4–1.8 cm, thickness 0.65–0.75 cm

Liaoning Provincial Institute of Cultural Relics and Archaeology

白色，大小、形制相近。均磨制，近扁平体，正面正中作一竖向通体凹槽，使贝的横截面近似凹字形。顶面平弧，磨出一小台面，沟槽两侧刻划多道平行短线，由槽内一面钻二通透小孔。使其形似贝壳，且可穿系。

227

龙 衍 九 州
The Dragon Hovers
over China

龙腾中国：红山文化古国文明
Legends of Dragon：
The Ancient Civilization of Hongshan Culture

166. 蛇形玉坠

红山文化（距今约 6500-5000 年）

2011 年辽宁省朝阳市凌源市田家沟墓地 9 号墓出土（M9:1）

长 8.4 厘米，宽 2.2 厘米，厚 1.2 厘米

辽宁省文物考古研究院藏

Snake-shaped Jade Pendant

Hongshan Culture (ca. 6,500–5,000 BP)

Unearthed from Tomb No. 9, Tianjiagou Cemetery, Lingyuan, Chaoyang, Liaoning in 2011 (M9:1)

Length 8.4 cm, width 2.2 cm, thickness 1.2 cm

Liaoning Provincial Institute of Cultural Relics and Archaeology

　　鸡骨白色透闪石玉，质地细腻莹润，器表附着埋藏土。器体呈扁薄长条状，一面略鼓，一面较平，一端圆弧如舌状微翘起，一端斜弧对穿一孔。雕琢如虫状，似蛇。隆起面刻划圆形双眼、如触角的弧线以及如虫身的瓦楞纹，舌状端刻划一道阴线似蛇虫口部，平整面刻划六道阴线。磨制精致，通体抛光。

167. 玉龟壳

红山文化（距今约 6500-5000 年）

1989 年辽宁省朝阳市建平县牛河梁遗址第二地点一号冢 21 号墓出土（N2Z1M21:10）

高 2.7 厘米，龟背长 5.3 厘米，宽 4.1 厘米，腹部残长 4.5 厘米，宽 3.8 厘米，圆凹径 2.3 厘米

辽宁省文物考古研究院藏

Jade Tortoise Shell

Hongshan Culture (ca. 6,500–5,000 BP)

Unearthed from Tomb No. 21, Stone Mound No.1, Locus No. 2, Niuheliang Site, Jianping, Chaoyang, Liaoning in 1989 (N2Z1M21:10)

Height 2.7 cm, length of shell 5.3 cm, width of shell 4.1 cm, length (remaining) of belly 4.5 cm, width of belly 3.8 cm, diameter of round indent 2.3 cm

Liaoning Provincial Institute of Cultural Relics and Archaeology

　　淡绿色玉，一侧边缘有褐色瑕斑。平面近椭圆形，首部稍窄，尾部稍宽。龟背隆起，背面以减地起三道竖脊，中脊高于两侧脊，龟背的周边磨薄，显示裙边。以阴线刻出龟背纹，裙边缘处刻划多道放射状短线，头与尾处背、腹甲作出凹口，腹甲凹口较宽，背甲以双阴线表现尾部，头部刻单短阴线，或显示头尾收缩于体内状。

229

龙衍九州
The Dragon Hovers
over China

龙腾中国：红山文化古国文明
Legends of Dragon：
The Ancient Civilization of Hongshan Culture

168. 玉龟背甲

新石器时代晚期

内蒙古自治区通辽市境内征集
长 10.5 厘米，外径 4.5 厘米
内蒙古博物院藏

Jade Tortoise Shell

Late Neolithic Age

Acquired from Tongliao, Inner Mongolia
Length 10.5 cm, outer diameter 4.5 cm
Inner Mongolia Museum

龙衍九州
The Dragon Hovers
over China

『何以中国』文物考古大展系列
"The Essence of China:" an Exhibition Series
of Cultural Relics and Archaeological Achievements

  优质透闪石，呈灰褐色。器身呈龟背甲形，周身微鼓，两端浑圆，阴刻网格纹，有通天大孔。孔壁虽经打磨，但旋痕隐约可见。器表满布不规则绺裂，有黑色沁，应为燎祭所致，俗称"火劫纹"。肖生玉器在我国南、北地区的史前考古文化墓葬中均有出土，如辽宁省建平县牛河梁遗址第二地点一号冢 21 号墓和安徽省含山县凌家滩遗址 4 号墓。这一时期的先民多通过龟背甲的大孔通神祈福。

以玉为尊

　　红山文化玉器作为随葬品，器类和组合体现墓主人生前社会等级、身份地位，一些特殊玉器仅见于高等
级墓葬，具有显著的专属性和标识性，成为红山文化玉礼器系统的突出特征。

169. 勾云形玉器残件

哈民文化（距今约 6000-5000 年）

2010-2012 年内蒙古自治区通辽市科尔沁左翼中旗哈民忙哈遗址 44 号房址出土

残长 5.0 厘米，宽 4.0 厘米，厚 0.4 厘米

内蒙古自治区文物考古研究院藏

231

龙　衍　九　州
The Dragon Hovers
over China

龙腾中国：红山文化古国文明
Legends of Dragon：
The Ancient Civilization of Hongshan Culture

Hooked-cloud-shaped Jade Object (incomplete)

Hamin Culture (ca. 6,000–5,000 BP)

Unearthed from House Remains No. 44, Hamin Mangha Site, Horqin Left Wing Middle Banner,

Tongliao, Inner Mongolia between 2010 and 2012

Length (remaining) 5.0 cm, width 4.0 cm, thickness 0.4 cm

Inner Mongolia Institute of Cultural Relics and Archaeology

　　闪透石质，黄绿色，半透明，整体近方形，雕琢精致。勾云形玉器仅存的一端应为原物
的二分之一。眼涡圆洼中心对穿，眼涡底下腮边及弯状镂空发达。上部为齿状突和上勾云，
下部为齿状突和下勾云组成。齿槽和齿口分别呈"U"字形和"V"字形。在眼涡边上下两处
对向穿孔，应是器物折断后的开孔，作捆绑之用。

170. 勾云形玉器

哈民文化（距今约 6000-5000 年）

2010-2012 年内蒙古自治区通辽市科尔沁左翼中旗哈民忙哈遗址 46 号房址出土

长 8.8 厘米，宽 3.2 厘米，厚 0.5 厘米

内蒙古自治区文物考古研究院藏

Hooked-cloud-shaped Jade Object

Hamin Culture (ca. 6,000–5,000 BP)

Unearthed from House Remains No. 46, Hamin Mangha Site, Horqin Left Wing Middle Banner,

Tongliao, Inner Mongolia between 2010 and 2012

Length 8.8 cm, width 3.2 cm, thickness 0.5 cm

Inner Mongolia Institute of Cultural Relics and Archaeology

　　闪透石质，通体黄色，整体呈圆角长方形。器身两面均有瓦沟纹，下沿中央有三个齿状突，上沿与短侧一端各有系孔，边缘呈刃状。

232

龙衍九州
The Dragon Hovers
over China

『何以中国』文物考古大展系列
"The Essence of China," an Exhibition Series
of Cultural Relics and Archaeological Achievements

171. 梳形玉器

哈民文化（距今约 6000-5000 年）

2010-2012 年内蒙古自治区通辽市科尔沁左翼中旗哈民忙哈遗址 47 号房址出土

长 6.19 厘米，宽 2.53 厘米，厚 0.58 厘米

内蒙古自治区文物考古研究院藏

Comb-shaped Jade Object

Hamin Culture (ca. 6,000–5,000 BP)

Unearthed from House Remains No. 47, Hamin Mangha Site, Horqin Left Wing Middle Banner,

Tongliao, Inner Mongolia between 2010 and 2012

Length 6.19 cm, width 2.53 cm, thickness 0.58 cm

Inner Mongolia Institute of Cultural Relics and Archaeology

　　浅黄绿色，为圆角长方形。器身正面下边弧状，无小齿状突，在中央部位有一对向穿破损的系孔，系孔邻近两侧再对向开两边系孔，左边破损，右边完整。系孔破损可能是使用中出现，其后在修复过程中，对下沿的边缘进行进一步加工。器身正面上边有三个齿状突，齿面上没开齿口，齿沟较浅。齿与齿之间为弧状瓦沟纹，直通到器物下边底部，短侧一端有系孔。器身反面基本磨平，中央有贯穿的条状螺旋纹的沟槽，可能与分割技术有关。

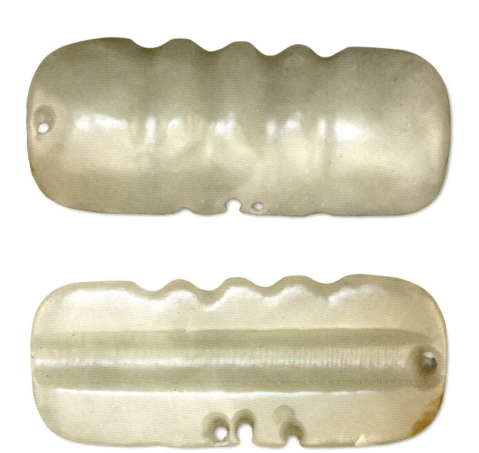

172. 勾云形玉器

红山文化（距今约 6500-5000 年）

1984 年辽宁省朝阳市建平县牛河梁遗址第二地点一号冢 9 号墓出土（N2Z1M9:2）

长 6.2 厘米，最宽 2.4 厘米，厚 0.4 厘米

辽宁省文物考古研究院藏

Hooked-cloud-shaped Jade Object

Hongshan Culture (ca. 6,500–5,000 BP)

Unearthed from Tomb No. 9, Stone Mound No.1, Locus No. 2, Niuheliang Site, Jianping, Chaoyang, Liaoning in 1984 (N2Z1M9:2)

Length 6.2 cm, greatest width 2.4 cm, thickness 0.4 cm

Liaoning Provincial Institute of Cultural Relics and Archaeology

龙 衍 九 州

The Dragon Hovers
over China

『何 以 中 国』文 物 考 古 大 展 系 列

"The Essence of China," an Exhibition Series
of Cultural Relics and Archaeological Achievements

　　淡绿色玉质。体小，体面平而无纹饰，仅在卷勾处稍有加工。通体呈扁平条状。两短侧边和一长侧边为圆弧形。另一长侧边较直，起三组 6 枚齿状突，齿突有残。体中部对穿双孔，上部对穿单孔。

173. 勾云形玉器

红山文化（距今约 6500-5000 年）

1989 年辽宁省朝阳市建平县牛河梁遗址第二地点一号冢 22 号墓出土（N2Z1M22：2）

长 14.2 厘米，宽 4.6 厘米，厚 0.45 厘米

辽宁省文物考古研究院藏

Hooked-cloud-shaped Jade Object

Hongshan Culture (ca. 6,500–5,000 BP)

Unearthed from Tomb No. 22, Stone Mound No.1, Locus No. 2, Niuheliang Site, Jianping, Chaoyang, Liaoning in 1989 (N2Z1M22:2)

Length 14.2 cm, width 4.6 cm, thickness 0.45 cm

Liaoning Provincial Institute of Cultural Relics and Archaeology

黄绿色玉质。呈长方形片状，一端宽，一端稍窄。有正反面之分，正面纹饰较为清晰。中部卷勾与器体相连，形成对称双孔，四角卷勾的勾体卷曲不显，勾端起尖。长边一侧作出五组齿状突，貌似兽面。出土于墓主人右胸侧。

174. 勾云形玉器

红山文化（距今约 6500-5000 年）

1994 年辽宁省朝阳市建平县牛河梁遗址第二地点一号冢 27 号墓出土（N2Z1M27：2）
长 28.6 厘米，宽 9.8 厘米，最厚 0.5 厘米
辽宁省文物考古研究院藏

Hooked-cloud-shaped Jade Object

Hongshan Culture (ca. 6,500–5,000 BP)

Unearthed from Tomb No. 27, Stone Mound No.1,Locus No. 2, Niuheliang Site, Jianping, Chaoyang, Liaoning in 1994 (N2Z1M27:2)
Length 28.6 cm, width 9.8 cm, greatest thickness 0.5 cm
Liaoning Provincial Institute of Cultural Relics and Archaeology

绿色玉质。片切割出料。呈长方形，为双勾形勾云形玉器。有正背面之分，体平而较薄，略弯向背面。整器以切片、甚浅的瓦沟纹、镂孔等工艺，刻画牙齿、双目和卷勾的造型。纹脊甚细而流畅。背面纹饰不够完整。近上沿中部一穿。出土位置在墓主头部的左侧、左肩以上，为竖置，背面朝上。此器形体规整，是牛河梁遗址出土玉器中个体最大，也是集高水平的切片、起地法、镂孔技法为一体的典型标本。

175. 勾云形玉器

红山文化（距今约 6500-5000 年）

1991 年辽宁省朝阳市建平县牛河梁遗址第二地点一号冢 24 号墓出土（N2Z1M24:3）

长 17.9 厘米，宽 10.8 厘米，厚 0.8 厘米

辽宁省文物考古研究院藏

Hooked-cloud-shaped Jade Object

Hongshan Culture (ca. 6,500–5,000 BP)

Unearthed from Tomb No. 24, Stone Mound No.1, Locus No. 2, Niuheliang Site, Jianping, Chaoyang, Liaoning in 1991 (N2Z1M24:3)

Length 17.9 cm, width 10.8 cm, thickness 0.8 cm

Liaoning Provincial Institute of Cultural Relics and Archaeology

237

龙 衍 九 州
The Dragon Hovers
over China

龙腾中国：红山文化古国文明
Legends of Dragon：
The Ancient Civilization of Hongshan Culture

　　绿色，泛黄，边缘有红褐色瑕斑，有裂纹。器体平面近于长方形，卷勾宽大，四角卷勾较为平直，仅尾部略呈钩形。有正、背面之分。正面有随卷勾走向的宽而浅的瓦沟纹。背面无纹饰。长边一侧居中近边缘处对钻双孔，孔间有系沟，以利穿绳佩戴。此器原已断为三块，两处残断面有磨痕，一处无，暗示此器非一次断裂，断裂处均有穿孔，似为锔孔之用。

176. 勾云形玉器

红山文化（距今约 6500-5000 年）

1985 年辽宁省朝阳市建平县牛河梁遗址第二地点一号冢 14 号墓出土（N2Z1M14:1）

长 15.8 厘米，宽 6.9 厘米，厚 0.6 厘米

辽宁省文物考古研究院藏

Hooked-cloud-shaped Jade Object

Hongshan Culture (ca. 6,500–5,000 BP)

Unearthed from Tomb No. 14, Stone Mound No.1, Locus No. 2, Niuheliang Site, Jianping, Chaoyang, Liaoning in 1985 (N2Z1M14:1)

Length 15.8 cm, width 6.9 cm, thickness 0.6 cm

Liaoning Provincial Institute of Cultural Relics and Archaeology

出土时已断为两段。质色白，通体磨光。略呈长方形。有正反面之分，反面平面无纹饰。从正面看，为中心镂空，作勾云形盘卷，卷勾边缘磨薄似刃，两长边均有两组齿突，齿突两侧各阴刻一较宽的短线，外四角卷勾，勾端点较圆。正面以减地磨出与卷勾走向相应的瓦沟纹，线条简洁流畅。近长边一侧残断处中间有一孔，两侧各一孔，为背面单钻，另一长边一侧近边缘处亦钻三孔，亦为残断处一孔，疑此器因钻孔而断裂，又穿铜孔以整合。

龙 衍 九 州
The Dragon Hovers
over China

『何以中国』文物考古大展系列
"The Essence of China," an Exhibition Series
of Cultural Relics and Archaeological Achievements

177. 勾云形玉器

红山文化（距今约 6500-5000 年）

1989 年辽宁省朝阳市建平县牛河梁遗址第二地点一号冢 21 号墓出土（N2Z1M21:3）

长 8.8 厘米，宽 4.3 厘米，孔径 1.2 厘米，厚 0.5 厘米

辽宁省文物考古研究院藏

Hooked-cloud-shaped Jade Object

Hongshan Culture (ca. 6,500–5,000 BP)

Unearthed from Tomb No. 21, Stone Mound No.1, Locus No. 2, Niuheliang Site, Jianping, Chaoyang, Liaoning in 1989 (N2Z1M21:3)

Length 8.8 cm, width 4.3 cm, diameter of hole 1.2 cm, thickness 0.5 cm

Liaoning Provincial Institute of Cultural Relics and Archaeology

淡绿色玉质，泛黄，一角有黄褐色瑕斑，较为光泽。体小，片状，无纹饰。中心只对钻一较大圆孔，长边有齿状突以显示为卷勾的末端。四角卷勾略显。边缘磨制为圆钝抹斜状。长边近缘斜钻一小孔。

239

龙衍九州
The Dragon Hovers
over China

龙腾中国：红山文化古国文明
Legends of Dragon :
The Ancient Civilization of Hongshan Culture

178. 勾云形玉器

红山文化（距今约 6500-5000 年）

辽宁省朝阳市凌源市牛河梁遗址采集

长 23.5 厘米，宽 11.3 厘米，厚 1.0 厘米

辽宁省博物馆藏

Hooked-cloud-shaped Jade Object

Hongshan Culture (ca. 6,500–5,000 BP)

Found at the Niuheliang Site, Lingyuan, Chaoyang, Liaoning

Length 23.5 cm, width 11.3 cm, thickness 1.0 cm

Liaoning Provincial Museum

　　此勾云形玉器为同类中体形较大、较为规整的一件。玉呈淡绿色，器表有土渍痕迹。体为长方板状，由中心及四角卷勾组成，上下、左右近乎对称。中部有弯弧状镂空，凸显一勾角。左右两侧各向外伸出一对勾角，弯曲不明显。上下两侧边缘处有两三个圆弧状凸起。有正背面的明显区分，正面琢磨出与形制相应的浅凹槽形纹路，背面平整、无纹饰。此类器物可能与玉斧钺功能类似。

　　勾云形玉器造型奇异，纹饰独特，具有极强的神秘色彩。该类玉器主要有三种形制：一种是长方形，四角呈现弯勾状；一种长条形，其中一个长边雕琢似齿状；还有一种是长条形的简化形式，体型较小。关于其原型，尚存争议。出土时多竖置于墓主胸部，反面朝上，推测与通神权杖有关。

179. 勾云形玉器

红山文化（距今约 6500-5000 年）

长 21.2 厘米，宽 11.2 厘米，厚 0.86 厘米

朝阳博物馆藏

Hooked-cloud-shaped Jade Object

Hongshan Culture (ca. 6,500–5,000 BP)

Length 21.2 cm, width 11.2 cm, thickness 0.86 cm

Chaoyang Museum

　　玉质不透明，赭红色，整体磨制抛光，器表局部有黄白色原岩斑和土渍痕。整体呈长方形片状，中部偏厚，边缘渐薄。器体正面微鼓，琢有浅凹槽纹，器身中部内琢一勾云状，四角有几乎对称向外弯曲的勾体。背面较为平整，分布有三组隧孔。

241

龙 衍 九 州
The Dragon Hovers
over China

龙腾中国：红山文化古国文明
Legends of Dragon :
The Ancient Civilization of Hongshan Culture

180. 勾云形玉器

红山文化（距今约 6500-5000 年）

长 13.7 厘米，宽 6.4 厘米，厚 0.75 厘米

故宫博物院藏

Hooked-cloud-shaped Jade Object

Hongshan Culture (ca. 6,500–5,000 BP)

Length 13.7 cm, width 6.4 cm, thickness 0.75 cm

The Palace Museum

　　淡黄绿色玉料，局部有褐色沁。呈长方形片状，中心透雕作勾云状，左右各一旋勾呈中心对称。上端有二凸脊，下端出三凸脊，四角有卷勾，两面磨出与内外轮廓相应的浅凹槽，边缘呈刃状。上部中间有一穿孔。这类玉器是红山文化玉器的重要器类，器型充满变化和动态之美，其形态存在想象、夸张和抽象的集合。它的用途目前尚无定论。此器上中部的穿孔可能用于穿系。此类玉器出土时发现多置于墓葬里人骨胸前的位置，由此推测，可能是佩系于胸前或作避邪用。

181. 勾云形玉器

红山文化（距今约 6500-5000 年）

长 14.0 厘米，宽 9.6 厘米，厚 0.47 厘米

朝阳博物馆藏

Hooked-cloud-shaped Jade Object

Hongshan Culture (ca. 6,500–5,000 BP)

Length 14.0 cm, width 9.6 cm, thickness 0.47 cm

Chaoyang Museum

透闪石玉质，黄绿色，半透明，玉质细密温润。器表有多处白色沁斑。器体呈薄片状，整体近似方形，中心部位镂空，作一勾云状卷角。外缘延伸出五个勾形，展现出多角勾云形。上部对钻一小孔，内外边缘均双面磨薄，器体中部均随器形走向磨制成凹陷的瓦沟纹。

龙腾中国：红山文化古国文明
Legends of Dragon :
The Ancient Civilization of Hongshan Culture

182. 勾云形玉器

红山文化（距今约 6500-5000 年）

长 10.8 厘米，宽 9.5 厘米

天津博物馆藏

Hooked-cloud-shaped Jade Object

Hongshan Culture (ca. 6,500–5,000 BP)

Length 10.8 cm, width 9.5 cm

Tianjin Museum

244

龙 衍 九 州
The Dragon Hovers
over China

『 何 以 中 国 』 文 物 考 古 大 展 系 列
"The Essence of China," an Exhibition Series
of Cultural Relics and Archaeological Achievements

　　青绿色玉质。片雕，两面纹饰基本相同。器近龟形，通体运用打洼工艺琢磨出浅凹槽，边缘磨出钝刃。器中和四周出勾云状卷勾，且卷勾方向一致，上部出廓并钻孔两个。该器工艺技法具红山文化典型特征。

183. 勾云形玉器

红山文化（距今约 6500-5000 年）

长 10.5 厘米，宽 7.1 厘米

天津博物馆藏

Hooked-cloud-shaped Jade Object

Hongshan Culture (ca. 6,500–5,000 BP)

Length 10.5 cm, width 7.1 cm

Tianjin Museum

245

龙行九州
The Dragon Hovers
over China

龙腾中国：红山文化古国文明
Legends of Dragon：
The Ancient Civilization of Hongshan Culture

　　深青色玉质。片雕，两面纹饰相同。器似龟，中间和出廓左右两边出不规则勾云形卷勾，器上端有两个凸起，中间钻孔两个，下端有凸起三个，整器边缘磨出钝刃。

184. 斜口筒形玉器

红山文化（距今约 6500-5000 年）

2014-2016 年辽宁省朝阳市半拉山墓地出土（JK12∶2）
通高 17.5 厘米，斜口长径 8.9 厘米，平口长径 7.5 厘米
辽宁省文物考古研究院藏

Cylindrical Jade Vessel with an Oblique Rim

Hongshan Culture (ca. 6,500–5,000 BP)

Unearthed from the Banlashan Cemetery, Chaoyang, Liaoning between 2014 and 2016 (JK12:2)
Overall height 17.5 cm, longer diameter of oblique rim 8.9 cm, longer diameter of flat rim 7.5 cm
Liaoning Provincial Institute of Cultural Relics and Archaeology

龙衍九州
The Dragon Hovers
over China

『何以中国』文物考古大展系列
"The Essence of China," an Exhibition Series
of Cultural Relics and Archaeological Achievements

深绿色玉石质，体表几乎布满白色沁斑。器体呈扁圆喇叭筒状。一端为稍窄小的平口，截面近椭圆形，两侧面近平口端各单面钻一细孔；一端为宽大的斜口，斜口外敞，截面近圆角梯形。斜口端外边缘磨薄似刃，边缘有破损疤痕。磨制光滑，略显光泽。

185. 斜口筒形玉器

红山文化（距今约 6500-5000 年）

2003 年辽宁省朝阳市凌源市牛河梁遗址第十六地点 10 号墓出土（N16M10:1）

通高 5.6 厘米，斜口长径 4.2 厘米，平口长径 3.3 厘米，壁厚 0.32 厘米

辽宁省文物考古研究院藏

Cylindrical Jade Vessel with an Oblique Rim

Hongshan Culture (ca. 6,500–5,000 BP)

Unearthed from Tomb No. 10, Locus No. 16, Niuheliang Site, Lingyuan, Chaoyang, Liaoning in 2003 (N16M10:1)

Overall height 5.6 cm, longer diameter of oblique rim 4.2 cm, longer diameter of flat rim 3.3 cm, thickness of wall 0.32 cm

Liaoning Provincial Institute of Cultural Relics and Archaeology

247

龙 衍 九 州
The Dragon Hovers
over China

龙腾中国：红山文化古国文明
Legends of Dragon：
The Ancient Civilization of Hongshan Culture

　　黄绿色玉质，局部偶见似皮壳的浅褐色瑕斑。器体呈扁圆筒状，中空，上粗下细。一端作斜口，腹壁外敞，另端作平口。斜口及平口端磨平，斜口略薄。内壁有钻孔痕迹和线切割痕迹。近底部长径两侧由外向内各钻一孔。

186. 斜口筒形玉器

红山文化（距今约 6500-5000 年）

1991 年辽宁省朝阳市建平县牛河梁遗址第二地点一号冢 25 号墓出土（N2Z1M25:6）

通高 11.1 厘米，斜口长径 8.7 厘米，平口长径 7.3 厘米，壁厚 0.4 厘米

辽宁省文物考古研究院藏

Cylindrical Jade Vessel with an Oblique Rim

Hongshan Culture (ca. 6,500–5,000 BP)

Unearthed from Tomb No. 25, Stone Mound No. 1, Locus No. 2, Niuheliang Site, Jianping, Chaoyang, Liaoning in 1991 (N2Z1M25:6)

Overall height 11.1 cm, longer diameter of oblique rim 8.7 cm, longer diameter of flat rim 7.3 cm, thickness of wall 0.4 cm

Liaoning Provincial Institute of Cultural Relics and Archaeology

绿色玉，有白色瑕斑。大斜口，斜口缘处磨成钝刃状，平口缘面平，近缘处钻对称双孔。内壁遗有加工时的线切割痕迹。出土时，器平置，平口朝向头部，短面和斜面朝上。

187. 斜口筒形玉器

红山文化（距今约 6500-5000 年）

1984 年辽宁省朝阳市建平县牛河梁遗址第二地点一号冢 4 号墓出土（N2Z1M4：1）

通高 18.6 厘米，斜口长径 10.7 厘米，平口长径 7.4 厘米，壁厚 0.3-0.7 厘米

辽宁省文物考古研究院藏

Cylindrical Jade Vessel with an Oblique Rim

Hongshan Culture (ca. 6,500–5,000 BP)

Unearthed from Tomb No. 4, Stone Mound No. 1, Locus No. 2, Niuheliang Site, Jianping, Chaoyang, Liaoning in 1984 (N2Z1M4:1)

Overall height 18.6 cm, longer diameter of oblique rim 10.7 cm, longer diameter of flat rim 7.4 cm, thickness of wall 0.3–0.7 cm

Liaoning Provincial Institute of Cultural Relics and Archaeology

深绿色玉质，质匀，通体内外磨光，光泽圆润。呈扁圆筒状。一端作平口，一端作斜口。斜口面较平而宽，面上稍显内凹。斜口外敞，口缘磨薄似刃状。平口两侧近边缘处各钻一小孔，以由外向内钻为主。内壁及上下端缘遗有用线切割法掏孔的痕迹，为由短边中部为起点，向两侧切割，由左到右占大半圈，由右到左占小半圈。

188. 斜口筒形玉器

红山文化（距今约 6500-5000 年）

1996 年辽宁省朝阳市建平县牛河梁遗址第二地点四号冢 9 号墓出土（N2Z4M9：1）

通高 12.7 厘米，斜口长径 9.0 厘米，平口长径 8.0 厘米，壁厚 0.2-0.5 厘米

辽宁省文物考古研究院藏

Cylindrical Jade Vessel with an Oblique Rim

Hongshan Culture (ca. 6,500–5,000 BP)

Unearthed from Tomb No. 9, Stone Mound No. 4, Locus No. 2, Niuheliang Site, Jianping, Chaoyang, Liaoning in 1996 (N2Z4M9:1)

Overall height 12.7 cm, longer diameter of oblique rim 9.0 cm, longer diameter of flat rim 8.0 cm, thickness of wall 0.2–0.5 cm

Liaoning Provincial Institute of Cultural Relics and Archaeology

深绿色玉，泛黄，有大片白色瑕斑。扁圆筒状，长面内凹不显，一端大斜口，平口一端为小斜口，口部边缘磨薄，斜口和平口边缘都遗有多处残缺痕，小斜口端可见掏孔芯时的钻痕。平口近端未见钻孔。出土于墓主人头顶左侧。

189. 斜口筒形玉器

红山文化（距今约 6500-5000 年）

1996 年辽宁省朝阳市建平县牛河梁遗址第二地点四号冢 15 号墓出土（N2Z4M15:2）

通高 9.96 厘米，斜口长径 8.4 厘米，平口长径 6.7 厘米，壁厚 0.1-0.55 厘米

辽宁省文物考古研究院藏

Cylindrical Jade Vessel with an Oblique Rim

Hongshan Culture (ca. 6,500–5,000 BP)

Unearthed from Tomb No. 15, Stone Mound No. 4, Locus No. 2, Niuheliang Site, Jianping, Chaoyang, Liaoning in 1996 (N2Z4M15:2)

Overall height 9.96 cm, longer diameter of oblique rim 8.4 cm, longer diameter of flat rim 6.7 cm, thickness of wall 0.1–0.55 cm

Liaoning Provincial Institute of Cultural Relics and Archaeology

淡绿色玉。扁圆筒状，一端斜口，一端为平口，斜口略大。平口处无小孔，斜口缘部略有残缺。长背内凹有弧度。平口边不齐，且斜向长面方向。出土于墓主人头顶，横置，短边朝上，平口朝北。

251

龙 衍 九 州
The Dragon Hovers
over China

龙腾中国：红山文化古国文明
Legends of Dragon：
The Ancient Civilization of Hongshan Culture

190. 斜口筒形玉器

红山文化（距今约 6500-5000 年）

1987 年辽宁省朝阳市建平县牛河梁遗址第二地点四号冢 2 号墓出土（N2Z4M2:1）

通高 17.2 厘米，斜口长径 9.7 厘米，平口长径 7.4 厘米，壁厚 0.6-0.8 厘米

辽宁省文物考古研究院藏

Cylindrical Jade Vessel with an Oblique Rim

Hongshan Culture (ca. 6,500–5,000 BP)

Unearthed from Tomb No. 2, Stone Mound No. 4, Locus No. 2, Niuheliang Site, Jianping, Chaoyang, Liaoning in 1987 (N2Z4M2:1)

Overall height 17.2 cm, longer diameter of oblique rim 9.7 cm, longer diameter of flat rim 7.4 cm, thickness of wall 0.6–0.8 cm

Liaoning Provincial Institute of Cultural Relics and Archaeology

252

龙 衍 九 州
The Dragon Hovers
over China

『何以中国』文物考古大展系列
"The Essence of China," an Exhibition Series
of Cultural Relics and Archaeological Achievements

绿色玉。扁圆筒状，一端作平口，一端作斜口，斜口端粗于平口端。斜口外敞，斜口靠长壁的一边较平，缘面磨制较薄，长壁微凹。平口缘面磨平或磨薄似刃。斜口内壁近中部有掏孔锃钻痕，平口内壁则显两处因线切割遗留的凹槽。平口端近底部两侧由外向内各钻一小孔。

191. 斜口筒形玉器

红山文化（距今约 6500-5000 年）

1996 年辽宁省朝阳市建平县牛河梁遗址第二地点四号冢 8 号墓出土（N2Z4M8：1）

通高 16.0 厘米，斜口长径 9.5 厘米，平口长径 7.4 厘米，壁厚 0.1-0.5 厘米

辽宁省文物考古研究院藏

Cylindrical Jade Vessel with an Oblique Rim

Hongshan Culture (ca. 6,500–5,000 BP)

Unearthed from Tomb No. 8, Stone Mound No. 4, Locus No. 2, Niuheliang Site, Jianping, Chaoyang, Liaoning in 1996 (N2Z4M8:1)

Overall height 16.0 cm, longer diameter of oblique rim 9.5 cm, longer diameter of flat rim 7.4 cm, thickness of wall 0.1–0.5 cm

Liaoning Provincial Institute of Cultural Relics and Archaeology

　　黄绿色玉，色较淡，有大片白色瑕斑，有裂纹。扁圆筒状，一端平口，一端作斜口，上下口边缘都磨薄似刃，平口缘部有残缺。长面微内凹，短面内壁右侧可见一道锃钻痕迹，直通上下。短面近底端两侧无钻孔。

192. 斜口筒形玉器

红山文化（距今约 6500-5000 年）

1988 年内蒙古自治区赤峰市敖汉旗烧锅地出土

通高 15.3 厘米，斜口长径 9.4 厘米，平口长径 7.5 厘米

敖汉博物馆（敖汉旗文物保护中心）藏

Cylindrical Jade Vessel with an Oblique Rim

Hongshan Culture (ca. 6,500–5,000 BP)

Unearthed from Shaoguodi Village, Aohan Banner, Chifeng, Inner Mongolia in 1988

Overall height 15.3 cm, longer diameter of oblique rim 9.4 cm, longer diameter of flat rim 7.5 cm

Aohan Museum (Aohan Banner Conservation Center of Cultural Relics)

黄色玉有红沁，通体抛光。质地较好。扁圆筒状，上粗下细。上端为斜口，腹壁略内弧，下端为平口。上、下端口边缘均有小残缺，壁较薄呈半透明状，内壁残存有线切割的弧形痕迹。

193. 斜口筒形玉器

红山文化（距今约 6500-5000 年）

内蒙古自治区赤峰市巴林左旗杨家营子镇出土

通高 12.8 厘米，斜口长径 8.3 厘米，平口长径 7.1 厘米

巴林左旗辽上京博物馆藏

Cylindrical Jade Vessel with an Oblique Rim

Hongshan Culture (ca. 6,500–5,000 BP)

Unearthed from Yangjiayingzi Town, Bairin Left Banner, Chifeng, Inner Mongolia

Overall height 12.8 cm, longer diameter of oblique rim 8.3 cm, longer diameter of flat rim 7.1 cm

Bairin Left Banner Upper Capital of the Liao Dynasty Museum

黄色玉，玉质较软，并有黑褐斑。椭圆筒形，向一侧弧，上端为斜口，下口平，两侧各穿一小孔。为研究筒形玉器的用途提供了信息。外壁磨光，内壁存弧形的线切痕。保存完整，壁薄而透光，制作规范，是同类筒形玉器中的上乘之作。

256

龙衍九州
The Dragon Hovers
over China

『何以中国』文物考古大展系列
"The Essence of China," an Exhibition Series
of Cultural Relics and Archaeological Achievements

194. 斜口筒形玉器半成品

红山文化（距今约 6500-5000 年）

1996 年辽宁省朝阳市建平县牛河梁遗址第二地点四号冢 15 号墓出土（N2Z4M15:5）
长 19.0 厘米，宽 10.3 厘米，厚 7.2 厘米
辽宁省文物考古研究院藏

Semi-finished Cylindrical Jade Vessel with an Oblique Rim

Hongshan Culture (ca. 6,500–5,000 BP)

Unearthed from Tomb No. 15, Stone Mound No. 4, Locus No. 2, Niuheliang Site, Jianping, Chaoyang, Liaoning in 1996 (N2Z4M15:5)

Length 19.0 cm, width 10.3 cm, thickness 7.2 cm

Liaoning Provincial Institute of Cultural Relics and Archaeology

　　淡绿色玉。实心体。通体素光。长面显平整，短面圆弧，两端边缘起棱锐，粗细不一，粗端作斜面，斜面稍圆鼓，细端面平，整体形状似斜口筒形玉器。长面中部有大片残损凹坑。出土于墓主人足下，横置，长面朝上，平面朝南。当是制作斜口筒形玉器的半成品。

195. 斜口筒形玉器内芯

红山文化（距今约 6500-5000 年）

1982 年内蒙古自治区赤峰市敖汉旗小东山出土
高 11.2 厘米，最宽 6.2 厘米，厚 3.3 厘米
敖汉博物馆（敖汉旗文物保护中心）藏

Core Gouged out during the Production of a Cylindrical Jade Vessel with an Oblique Rim

Hongshan Culture (ca. 6,500–5,000 BP)

Unearthed from the Eastern Hill, Aohan Banner, Chifeng, Inner Mongolia in 1982

Height 11.2 cm, greatest width 6.2 cm, thickness 3.3 cm

Aohan Museum (Aohan Banner Conservation Center of Cultural Relics)

257

龙 衍 九 州
The Dragon Hovers
over China

龙腾中国：红山文化古国文明
Legends of Dragon：
The Ancient Civilization of Hongshan Culture

碧绿色玉，含黄白色絮状物，通体抛光。亚腰状，一端较窄较平，一端较宽圆弧。器身背面存有一纵向的凹槽，一端较尖，尖端有两处圆窝，均有线割的弧线痕。

龙脉　Legacy through the Ages

258

龙衍九州
The Dragon Hovers
over China

『何以中国』文物考古大展系列
"The Essence of China," an Exhibition Series
of Cultural Relics and Archaeological Achievements

　　玉龙是红山文化玉器群中最典型的器类之一，是红山社会龙图腾崇拜的主要载体，寄托了红山先民共同的精神信仰，代表了红山社会统一认同的形成。红山文化玉龙是中华龙的本源，对商、西周、东周时期蜷体玉龙的造型产生了直接影响，是中华五千年文明形成的重要标志之一。

　　Arguably the most notable type of Hongshan jade artifact, the jade dragon was the main vehicle for dragon totem worship in Hongshan society. It embodied the spirit and beliefs shared by the local people and signified the formation of a unified identity within their community. As the prototype of the Chinese dragon, the Hongshan jade dragon had a direct impact on the coiled jade dragon of the Shang, Western Zhou, and Eastern Zhou periods. Indeed, it is one of the key markers of the very beginning of Chinese civilization, which occurred more than five thousand years ago.

196. 玦形玉龙

红山文化（距今约 6500-5000 年）

2006 年辽宁省建平县东山岗墓地出土
高 4.12 厘米，宽 3.04 厘米，厚 1.02 厘米
辽宁省文物考古研究院藏

Jade Dragon in the Shape of *Jue* (slit ring)

Hongshan Culture (ca. 6,500–5,000 BP)

Unearthed from the Dongshangang Cemetery, Jianping, Chaoyang, Liaoning in 2006
Height 4.12 cm, width 3.04 cm, thickness 1.02 cm
Liaoning Provincial Institute of Cultural Relics and Archaeology

　　鸡骨白色玉石质，局部有黄色沁和黑色斑点，质地较细腻，通体磨制光滑。龙体卷曲如环，头尾相接。环孔由两侧对钻而成，对钻稍有偏差，孔缘经打磨。龙体无纹饰，龙首长立耳，耳廓宽大高耸。双目圆睁、微鼓，吻部前凸下探，一端与尾相接，两侧长鼻孔微张，嘴紧闭。

197. 玦形玉龙

红山文化（距今约 6500-5000 年）

1984 年辽宁省朝阳市建平县牛河梁遗址第二地点一号冢 4 号墓出土（N2Z1M4:2）

高 10.3 厘米，宽 7.8 厘米，厚 3.3 厘米

辽宁省文物考古研究院藏

Jade Dragon in the Shape of *Jue* (slit ring)

Hongshan Culture (ca. 6,500–5,000 BP)

Unearthed from Tomb No. 4, Stone Mound No. 1, Locus No. 2, Niuheliang Site, Jianping, Chaoyang, Liaoning in 1984 (N2Z1M4:2)

Height 10.3 cm, width 7.8 cm, thickness 3.3 cm

Liaoning Provincial Institute of Cultural Relics and Archaeology

259

龙 衍 九 州
The Dragon Hovers
over China

龙腾中国：红山文化古国文明
Legends of Dragon：
The Ancient Civilization of Hongshan Culture

淡绿色玉质，微泛黄。通体精磨，光泽圆润。背及底部有红褐色沁色，背面沁色面积较大，颜色尤重，且不够光滑，疑为河磨玉的皮壳部分。龙体卷曲如环，头尾切开又似玦。体扁圆而厚，环孔由两侧对钻，呈圆形，边缘磨光。背上部钻单孔，孔缘不规则。兽首形，短立耳宽厚肥大，两耳之间从额中到头顶起短棱脊。目圆而稍鼓，目的圆度略不规则，吻部前突，有鼻孔，口略张开。

198. 玦形玉龙

红山文化（距今约 6500-5000 年）

2003 年辽宁省朝阳市凌源市牛河梁遗址第十六地点 14 号墓出土（N16M14:3）
高 9.69 厘米，宽 7.62 厘米，中孔径 1.93-2.21 厘米，小孔径 0.39-0.81 厘米，厚 2.61 厘米
辽宁省文物考古研究院藏

Jade Dragon in the Shape of *Jue* (slit ring)

Hongshan Culture (ca. 6,500–5,000 BP)

Unearthed from Tomb No. 14, Locus No. 16, Niuheliang Site, Lingyuan, Chaoyang, Liaoning in 2003 (N16M14:3)
Height 9.69 cm, width 7.62 cm, diameter of central hole 1.93–2.21 cm, diameter of smaller hole 0.39–0.81 cm, thickness 2.61 cm
Liaoning Provincial Institute of Cultural Relics and Archaeology

淡绿色玉质，微泛黄，耳部见有土黄色斑沁，背部有裂纹，背和底部遗有原玉料凹坑点。
质较匀。体扁圆厚重，卷曲呈椭圆形，首尾切开形似玦。头部较大，前额微凸，两个圆弧状
立耳稍向外撇。双耳间起棱脊。面部以阴线雕出圆目、口及吻部皱折，吻部前凸。长圆形鼻孔，
鼻孔上下各三道皱折。嘴紧闭。所施线条甚浅。颈部穿一圆孔。

龙 衍 九 州
The Dragon Hovers
over China

『何 以 中 国』文 物 考 古 大 展 系 列
"The Essence of China," an Exhibition Series
of Cultural Relics and Archaeological Achievements

199. 玦形玉龙

红山文化（距今约 6500-5000 年）

1984 年辽宁省朝阳市建平县张福店村采集
高 14.1 厘米，宽 10.2 厘米，厚 4.0 厘米
辽宁省文物考古研究院藏

Jade Dragon in the Shape of *Jue* (slit ring)

Hongshan Culture (ca. 6,500–5,000 BP)

Found at Zhangfudian Village, Jianping, Chaoyang, Liaoning in 1984
Height 14.1 cm, width 10.2 cm, thickness 4.0 cm
Liaoning Provincial Institute of Cultural Relics and Archaeology

淡绿色玉。环体，较扁平，缺口未切透，缘相连，切口为平口，大小孔都为两面对钻。以阴线刻出目、鼻，线条粗细不匀，以中部线条较粗，由中部向两侧渐由粗到细，且线条较短，有多处接头，有的接头或错开或相交。

261

龙 衍 九 州
The Dragon Hovers
over China

龙腾中国：红山文化古国文明
Legends of Dragon:
The Ancient Civilization of Hongshan Culture

200. 玦形玉龙

红山文化（距今约 6500-5000 年）

1980 年内蒙古自治区赤峰市巴林右旗那日斯台遗址出土
高 7.3 厘米，宽 5.1 厘米，厚 2.7 厘米
巴林右旗博物馆藏

Jade Dragon in the Shape of *Jue* (slit ring)

Hongshan Culture (ca. 6,500–5,000 BP)

Unearthed from the Narisitai Site, Bairin Right Banner, Chifeng, Inner Mongolia in 1980
Height 7.3 cm, width 5.1 cm, thickness 2.7 cm
Bairin Right Banner Museum

龙 衍 九 州
The Dragon Hovers
over China

『何以中国』文物考古大展系列

"The Essence of China," an Exhibition Series
of Cultural Relics and Archaeological Achievements

　　黄玉质地，龙身蜷曲呈头尾相对式，头部较大，额头隆起，圆弧形双耳竖起，隐地凸起
的一对大圆眼睛极具神韵，下额前伸，吻部凸出。用砣具将唇、眉、鼻等部位以阴刻线琢出
轮廓，线条流畅，磨制光滑。颈部对穿一圆孔，内视有平行旋转的螺旋纹。尾端圆收呈细尖状，
器身光素无纹。局部有红褐色沁斑。

201. 玦形玉龙

红山文化（距今约 6500-5000 年）

1987 年内蒙古自治区赤峰市敖汉旗河西出土
高 7.3 厘米，宽 5.6 厘米，孔径 1.7-1.9 厘米，小孔径 0.3-0.6 厘米
敖汉博物馆（敖汉旗文物保护中心）藏

Jade Dragon in the Shape of *Jue* (slit ring)

Hongshan Culture (ca. 6,500–5,000 BP)

Unearthed from Hexi Village, Aohan Banner, Chifeng, Inner Mongolia in 1987
Height 7.3 cm, width 5.6 cm, diameter of hole 1.7–1.9 cm, diameter of smaller hole 0.3–0.6 cm
Aohan Museum (Aohan Banner Conservation Center of Cultural Relics)

龙 衍 九 州
The Dragon Hovers
over China

『何以中国』文物考古大展系列
"The Essence of China," an Exhibition Series
of Cultural Relics and Archaeological Achievements

　　黄绿色玉，有红褐色斑沁，通体抛光。兽首，玦形身。头部较大，双耳呈圆弧状竖起，双耳至顶部有一道棱脊。前额微突，圆目，菱形突睛，嘴前伸，身体卷曲。颈部小孔对穿，有磨损痕。中部大孔，孔壁抛光，孔缘起棱。缺口有切割痕。

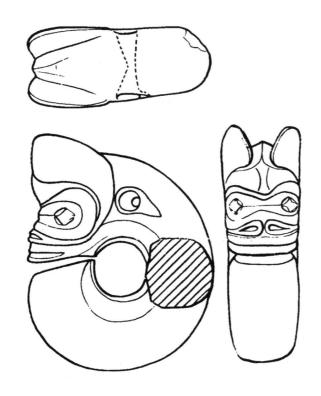

202. 玦形玉龙

红山文化（距今约 6500-5000 年）

1983 年内蒙古自治区赤峰市敖汉旗大五家村西出土

高 5.1 厘米，宽 5.0 厘米，厚 2.6 厘米

敖汉博物馆（敖汉旗文物保护中心）藏

Jade Dragon in the Shape of *Jue* (slit ring)

Hongshan Culture (ca. 6,500–5,000 BP)

Unearthed from a site west to Dawujia Village, Aohan Banner, Chifeng, Inner Mongolia in 1983

Height 5.1 cm, width 5.0 cm, thickness 2.6 cm

Aohan Museum (Aohan Banner Conservation Center of Cultural Relics)

266

龙 衍 九 州

The Dragon Hovers
over China

『何 以 中 国』 文物考古大展系列

"The Essence of China," an Exhibition Series
of Cultural Relics and Archaeological Achievements

碧绿色玉，夹杂白色斑点并显露表皮，通体抛光。兽首，玦形身。双耳后扬，耳尖部磨平。前额略突，圆目，嘴较长且前伸，身体卷曲。中部大孔壁较直磨光，颈部小孔两面穿。

203. 玦形玉龙

红山文化（距今约 6500-5000 年）

内蒙古自治区赤峰市巴林左旗尖山子村出土
高 8.2 厘米，宽 6.2 厘米，厚 3.4 厘米
巴林左旗辽上京博物馆藏

Jade Dragon in the Shape of *Jue* (slit ring)

Hongshan Culture (ca. 6,500–5,000 BP)

Unearthed from Jianshanzi Village, Bairin Left Banner, Chifeng, Inner Mongolia
Height 8.2 cm, width 6.2 cm, thickness 3.4 cm
Bairin Left Banner Upper Capital of the Liao Dynasty Museum

灰白色玉，有黑色纹理和斑点。头部大，厚双耳，双目圆睁，目下饰以沟槽纹龙嘴。卷躯，耳后对穿一圆孔，孔内磨痕清晰，系穿绳佩戴或悬挂所致，造型浑厚，神态凝重。

267

龙 衍 九 州
The Dragon Hovers
over China

龙腾中国：红山文化古国文明
Legends of Dragon：
The Ancient Civilization of Hongshan Culture

204. 玦形玉龙

红山文化（距今约 6500-5000 年）

高 15.1 厘米，宽 10.0 厘米，厚 4.2 厘米

朝阳博物馆藏

Jade Dragon in the Shape of *Jue* (slit ring)

Hongshan Culture (ca. 6,500–5,000 BP)

Height 15.1 cm, width 10.0 cm, thickness 4.2 cm

Chaoyang Museum

透闪石玉质，黄绿色，通体抛光，杂红褐、墨色。龙体下部及脊背处受黄、白色沁。龙体形呈扁圆形卷体，体中对钻一圆形穿孔。首、尾处自外向内切割略呈玦式口，形成龙嘴。龙首较大，额、鼻部前凸，双耳宽硕高耸，复线阴刻圆形双目，减地打洼琢刻椭圆形双鼻孔及吻部褶皱，颈背处对穿一小圆孔。

269

龙 衍 九 州
The Dragon Hovers
over China

龙腾中国∷红山文化古国文明
Legends of Dragon∷
The Ancient Civilization of Hongshan Culture

205. 玦形玉龙

红山文化（距今约 6500-5000 年）

高 9.54 厘米，宽径 7.08 厘米，中孔径 2.0 厘米，小孔径 1.88 厘米，厚 2.95 厘米

朝阳博物馆藏

Jade Dragon in the Shape of *Jue* (slit ring)

Hongshan Culture (ca. 6,500–5,000 BP)

Height 9.54 cm, width 7.08 cm, diameter of central hole 2.0 cm, diameter of smaller hole 1.88 cm, thickness 2.95 cm

Chaoyang Museum

透闪石玉质，青黄色，通体精磨抛光，龙体蜷曲，中央大孔为两侧对钻，孔缘经磨光，颈背部对钻一小穿孔，龙首部比例匀称丰满，阔耳尖耸，圆目微鼓，吻部前凸，嘴微张，面部以流畅的阴线刻出圆目、额纹、口、齿、及颚与吻上的褶皱，器表有部分土沁。

271

龙　衍　九　州
The Dragon Hovers
over China

龙腾中国：红山文化古国文明
Legends of Dragon：
The Ancient Civilization of Hongshan Culture

206. 玦形玉龙

红山文化（距今约 6500-5000 年）

高 14.0 厘米，宽 9.5 厘米

天津博物馆藏

Jade Dragon in the Shape of *Jue* (slit ring)

Hongshan Culture (ca. 6,500–5,000 BP)

Height 14.0 cm, width 9.5 cm

Tianjin Museum

玉质深绿色。器形硕大，首与尾相接处未断，内缘相连。头部有宽厚双立耳，采用阴刻兼打洼技法雕琢圆目和褶皱的鼻梁，唇部稍显凸出，颈部有对钻孔两个，这一点在同类文物中较少见。整器造型大气古朴。

207. 玦形玉龙

红山文化（距今约 6500-5000 年）

高 6.8 厘米，厚 2.1 厘米

上海博物馆藏

Jade Dragon in the Shape of *Jue* (slit ring)

Hongshan Culture (ca. 6,500–5,000 BP)

Height 6.8 cm, thickness 2.1 cm

Shanghai Museum

玉质呈绿色，表面大部布满斑驳的赭褐色。圆雕，头似熊，双圈大眼，凸鼻，闭嘴，圆凹耳，身躯弯曲，首、尾原衔接，现稍有断损，颈部处穿一孔。

208. "C"形玉龙

红山文化（距今约 6500-5000 年）

高 25.7 厘米，最宽 21.8 厘米，曲长 64.3 厘米，直径 1.9-3.0 厘米。

故宫博物院藏

C-shaped Jade Dragon

Hongshan Culture (ca. 6,500–5,000 BP)

Height 25.7 cm, greatest width 21.8 cm, length of arc 64.3 cm, diameter 1.9–3.0 cm

The Palace Museum

龙 衍 九 州

The Dragon Hovers
over China

『何以中国』文物考古大展系列

"The Essence of China," an Exhibition Series
of Cultural Relics and Archaeological Achievements

一整块黄绿色的闪石玉雕琢而成，有着优美的虹形曲线。头部雕琢，单阴线眼似梭形，大而凸出。吻部长而前凸，鼻上翘，下颚有两道阴线纹。脑后长鬣飘逸，神气生动，边缘呈刃状。龙身呈长圆柱形，光素，无肢无爪，无角无鳞，躯体似蛇，弯成"C"形弯钩，遒劲有力。中部有穿系孔。

"C"形龙是目前发现玉器中龙的最早形态之一，也是最符合人们头脑中龙的形象的玉器，但对其造型来源却有多种说法：有学者认为其祖形的最初来源与猪首有关；也有人认为，此龙的祖型为马首形，长鬣看更近似于马，极似草原奔马；还有人认为是多种动物的集合体。无论如何，大家均不约而同地将其定名为龙，是最早的被公认的玉质龙。这件"C"形玉龙简约、神秘，是史前红山人的神灵崇拜物，也是中华龙文化的源泉之一。

指导单位

上海市文化和旅游局　辽宁省文化和旅游厅　内蒙古自治区文化和旅游厅　河北省文化和旅游厅

主办单位

上海博物馆　辽宁省文物考古研究院　辽宁省博物馆　内蒙古自治区文物考古研究院

内蒙古博物院　河北省文物考古研究院

协办单位（按首字笔画排序）

天津博物馆　中国国家博物馆　巴林左旗辽上京博物馆　巴林右旗博物馆　辽宁大学　赤峰学院　赤峰博物院

张家口市宣化区文物管理所　阿鲁科尔沁旗博物馆　故宫博物院　敖汉博物馆（敖汉旗文物保护中心）

翁牛特旗博物馆（翁牛特旗文物保护中心）　朝阳博物馆　喀喇沁左翼蒙古族自治县博物馆　滦平县博物馆

总策划

褚晓波

学术顾问

高蒙河　贾笑冰　白宝玉

内容策划

陈杰　黄翔　马晓光　冯雨程

统筹协调

褚馨　金科羽　赵佳　王幸立　林文思

陈列设计

杜超

运输协调

韦刚

文物预防性保护

黄河　丁忠明　徐方圆

展品撰写（按姓氏笔画排序）

于晓婷　马卉　王宇　王铁华　任君宇　刘梦媛　刘铭　孙明明　孙斯琴格日乐　阮国利

苏都毕力格　沈莎莎　张尉　陈钟　邵雯　孟令婧　赵玉亮　徐琳　高阳　唐洁

萨如拉　商原驰　温科学　解曜珲　樊圣英　魏巍

展品摄影（按姓氏笔画排序）

厉恩杰　白羽　冯吉祥　冯辉　刘志岗　苏都毕力格　李健　沙大禹　沙楚清

张博程　武进新　庞雷　胡锤　高阳　薛皓冰

英文翻译与审校

孙欣祺　章吉　赵佳　金科羽　王幸立

图书在版编目（CIP）数据

龙腾中国 ：红山文化古国文明 / 上海博物馆编.

上海 ： 上海书画出版社，2025. 6.

-- ISBN 978-7-5479-3599-6

Ⅰ. K871.132

中国国家版本馆CIP数据核字第2025JP2179号

龙腾中国：红山文化古国文明

上海博物馆　编

主　　编	褚晓波
责任编辑	王　彬　金国明
特约编辑	丁唯涵
审　　读	陈家红
特约审读	陈　凌
装帧设计	张晶晶
图文制作	白瑾怡
技术编辑	包赛明

出版发行	上 海 世 纪 出 版 集 团 上海书画出版社
地　　址	上海市闵行区号景路159弄A座4楼
邮政编码	201101
网　　址	www.shshuhua.com
E - m a i l	shuhua@shshuhua.com
设计制作	上海汉唐晟源艺术设计有限公司
印　　刷	上海雅昌艺术印刷有限公司
经　　销	各地新华书店
开　　本	635×965　1/8
印　　张	35
版　　次	2025年6月第1版　2025年6月第1次印刷

书　　号	ISBN 978-7-5479-3599-6
定　　价	380.00元

若有印刷、装订质量问题，请与承印厂联系